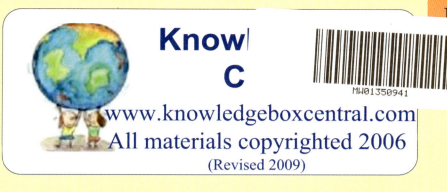

www.knowledgeboxcentral.com
All materials copyrighted 2006
(Revised 2009)

Welcome to our "Exploring Creation With Zoology 1: Flying Creatures of the Fifth Day" Lapbook Package (Lessons 1-14)

Designed by Dr. Cyndi Kinney with expressed permission from Apologia Science and Jeannie Fulbright

This is the "Pre-Printed Do-It-Yourself" format of this product.

The templates have been printed on paper that is colored specifically to improve information retention, as determined by scientific research.

This lapbook package includes 2 lapbooks which have been specifically designed for use with the book, by Jeannie Fulbright and Apologia Science.

This package includes one lapbook that covers Lessons 1 – 6, and another lapbook that covers Lessons 7-14.

Welcome to our "Exploring Creation With Zoology 1: Flying Creatures of the Fifth Day" Lapbook Package (Lessons 1-14)

On the following pages, you will find 2 separate lapbooks. First, you will find a lapbook that covers lessons 1-6. Next, you will find a lapbook that covers lessons 7-14.

If you have any questions regarding lapbook assembly, please feel free to contact us. You may email Cyndi at Cyndi@knowledgeboxcentral.com.

Thanks so much for your purchase. We would love to see pictures of your completed product! Please consider emailing them to us for inclusion in our newsletters and/or website.

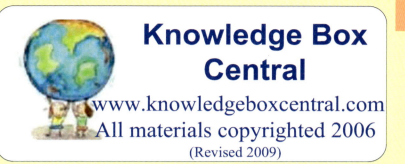

L_FCFD1_D

Welcome to our "Exploring Creation With Zoology 1: Flying Creatures of the Fifth Day" Lapbook (Lessons 1 – 6)

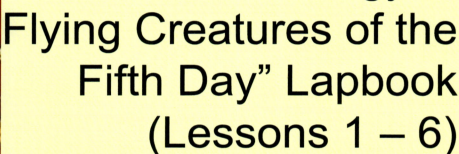

Designed by Dr. Cyndi Kinney with expressed permission from Apologia Science and Jeannie Fulbright

Exploring Creation with Zoology 1: *Flying Creatures of the Fifth Day* (Lessons 1 – 6) Lapbook.
This lapbook has been specifically designed for use with the book, by Jeannie Fulbright and Apologia Science.

This lapbook covers Lessons 1 – 6, and lessons 7 – 14 are covered in a separate lapbook.

This is the "Pre-Printed Do-It-Yourself" format of this product.

The templates have been printed on paper that is colored specifically to improve information retention, as determined by scientific research.

"Exploring Creation With Zoology 1: Flying Creatures of the Fifth Day" Lapbook for Lessons 1-6

Published by :

Knowledge Box Central
155 Clements Rd.
Plain Dealing, La. 71064

All information and graphics within this product are originals or have been used with permission from its owners, and credit has been given when appropriate. These include, but are not limited to the following: www.iclipart.com, and Art Explosion Clipart.

All rights reserved. No part of this book may be reproduced or transmitted in any form or by any means, electronic or mechanical, including photocopying, recording or by any information storage and retrieval system without written permission from the author. The Ebook and Cd Rom Formats are licensed for use by ONLY the household family of the purchaser of the product, allowing for copies to be made for each child within THAT household ONLY. "Pre-Printed/Do-It-Yourself" formats may NOT be copied. These are meant to be used for 1 student ONLY. "Pre-Assembled" formats may NOT be copied in any way and are also meant to be used for 1 student ONLY. Any violation of this policy is also a violation of the United States Copyright Laws.

If you have any questions regarding this copyright/licensure agreement, please contact cyndi@knowledgeboxcentral.com.

Copyright © 2009 Knowledge Box Central

www.knowledgeboxcentral.com

Printed in the United States of America

PLEASE NOTE: This is the first of 2 lapbooks for this book, "Exploring Creation With Zoology 1: Flying Creatures of the Fifth Day."

This particular lapbook ONLY covers Lessons 1 through 6.
You will need BOTH lapbooks in order to complete the entire book in lapbook format.

How do I get started?

First, you will want to gather your supplies.

*** Assembly:

    *Folders: We use colored file folders, which can be found at Walmart, Sam's, Office Depot, Costco, etc. You will need between 2 and 4 file folders, depending on which product you have purchased. You may use manilla folders if you prefer, but we have found that children respond better with the brightly colored folders. Don't worry about the tabs….they aren't important. *If you prefer, you can purchase the assembled lapbook bases from our website.*

    *Glue: For the folder assembly, we use hot glue. For booklet assembly, we use glue sticks and sometimes hot glue, depending on the specific booklet. We have found that bottle glue stays wet for too long, so it's not a great choice for lapbooking.

    *Other Supplies: Of course, you will need scissors. Many booklets require additional supplies. Some of these include metal brad fasteners, paper clips, ribbon, yarn, staples, hole puncher, etc. You may want to add decorations of your own, including stickers, buttons, coloring pages, cut-out clipart, etc. The most important thing is to use your imagination! Make it your own!!

Ok. I've gathered the supplies. Now how do I use this product?

Inside, you will find several sections. They are as follows:

1. **Lapbook Assembly Guide:** This section is written directly to the student, in language that he or she can understand. However, depending on the age of the child, there may be some parent/teacher assistance needed. These instructions will tell the student exactly how to assemble the lapbook base and how to cut out and assemble each booklet. Here, they will find a layout of where each booklet should be placed in the lapbook and pictures of a completed lapbook. They will also tell the student exactly what should be written inside each booklet as he or she comes to it during the study.

2. **Teacher's Guide:** This section is a great resource for the parent/teacher. In this section, you will find the page number where each answer may be found in the book. You will also find suggestions of extra activities that you may want to use with your student.

3. **Templates:** This section includes ALL of the templates for the booklets. These have been printed on colors that will help to improve retention of the information presented, according to scientific research on color psychology.

Exploring Creation With Zoology 1:
Flying Creatures of the Fifth Day Lessons 1 - 6
Lapbook Assembly Guide

You will need 3 folders of any color. Take each one and fold both sides toward the original middle fold and make firm creases on these folds (Figure 1). Then glue (and staple if needed) the backs of the small flaps together (Figure 2).

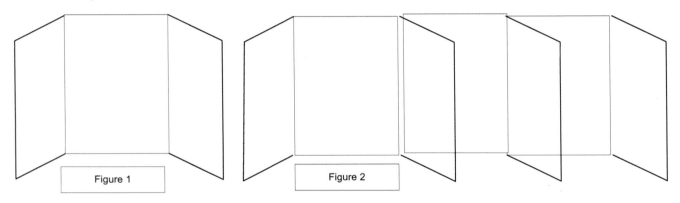

This is the "Layout" for your lapbook. The shapes are not exact on the layout, but you will get the idea of where each booklet should go inside your lapbook.

Inside of 1st Folder:

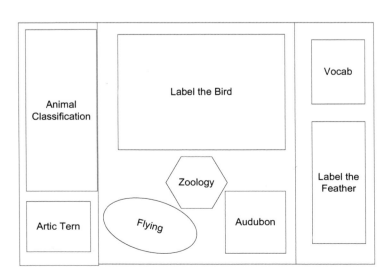

Inside of 2nd Folder:

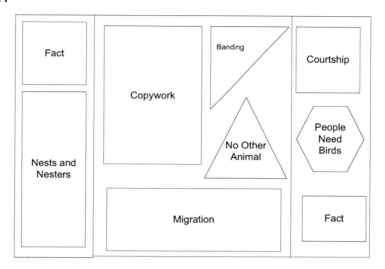

Inside of 3rd Folder:

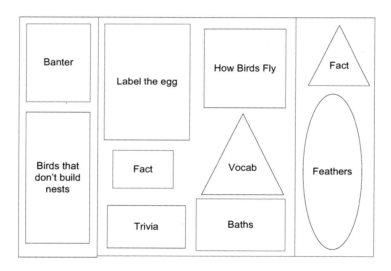

We have added pictures of a completed lapbook!!! This should help in figuring out how to assemble the booklets and then how to put it all together!

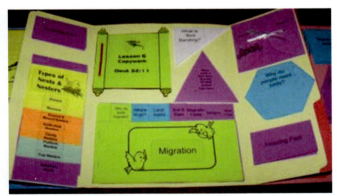

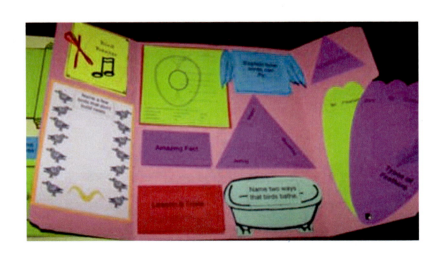

Flying Creatures of the Fifth Day Lessons 1 - 6
Lapbook Assembly Guide

Inside of 1st Folder:
1.   Animal Classification Booklet: Cut out along the outer black line edges of the booklet and the text boxes (2nd page). Glue the text boxes on the back of the booklet, and then tri-fold the booklet, so that a blank is on the back, and the title is on the front.
2.   Arctic Tern Booklet: Cut out along the outer black line edges. Then, accordion-fold the booklet, so that the title is on the front.
3.   Label the Bird Booklet: Cut out along the outer black line edges. Then, mount on a slightly larger piece of paper of a different color, creating a thin border around the edges.
4.   Zoology Booklet: Cut out along the outer black line edges. Then, fold along the center line so that the title is on the front.
5.   Flying Booklet: Cut out along the outer black line edges of all 6 pages. Then, stack them together, with the title page on the top. Punch a small hole in the end of the "wing," and be sure that it goes through the entire stack. Then secure together with a metal brad fastener.
6.   Audubon Booklet: Cut out along the outer black line edges, and then fold along the center line so that the title and graphic are on the front.
7.   Lesson 1 Vocabulary Booklet: Cut out along the outer black line edges of the booklet. This will be in a "L" shape. Fold the portion that is on the right (bottom of the 'L') over on top of the section to its left. Now, you will have just a straight line in the shape of an "I." Now, accordion-fold the booklet so that the title is on the front.
8.   "Label the Feather" Booklet: Cut out along the outer black line edges. Then, mount on a slightly larger piece of paper of a different color, creating a small border.

Inside of 2nd t Folder:
1.   Amazing Fact Booklets (2): Cut out along the outer black line edges of the booklet, and then fold along the center line so that the title is on the front.
2.   Migration Booklet: Cut out along the outer black line edges of each page. Note that you will have a larger "tab" at the top of each page. Stack them together, so that the title is on the front, and the "tabs" get progressively larger as you move toward the back of the booklet. You may secure along the left side of the booklet with staples, punched holes/ribbon, or punched holes/metal brad fasteners. See pictures.
3.   Types of Nests & Nesters Booklet: Cut out along the outer black line edges of each page. Then, stack them together, with the title on top and with each page getting progressively longer and creating "tabs." Staple twice at the top of the stack.
4.   "What Does A Bird Have…" Booklet: Cut out along the outer black line edges. Then, fold along the center line so that the title is on the front.

5. Lesson 6 Copywork Booklet: Cut out along the outer black line edges of each page. Stack together, with the title on top and the verse and blank pages following. Punch 2 holes along the left side, and secure with ribbon.
6. Banding Booklet: Cut out along the outer black line edges of the booklet, and fold along the center line so that the title is on the front.
7. Courtship Rituals Booklet: Cut out along the outer black line edges of the booklet. Fold along the vertical lines, so that the rounded edges almost meet, with the words on the outside. Punch a hole through each small circle, and tie a ribbon in a bow to secure the "flaps" together.
8. "Birds Need People" Booklet: Cut out along the outer black line edges, and fold along the center line so that the title is on the front.

Inside of 3rd Folder:
1. Bird Banter Booklet: Cut out along the outer black line edges of all pages. Then, stack on top of each other, with the title on the top. Punch 2 holes along the left edge, and secure with a ribbon.
2. "Birds that don't build nests" Booklet: Cut out along the outer black line edges, and then mount on a slightly larger piece of paper of a different color, so that you have a small border.
3. Amazing Fact Booklets (2): Cut out along the outer black line edges. Then, fold along the center line so that the title is on the front.
4. "Label the Egg" Booklet: Cut out along the outer black line edges, and then mount on a slightly larger piece of paper of a different color, so that you have a small border.
5. Lesson 6 Trivia Booklet: Cut out along the outer black line edges of the booklet. Then, fold the bottom section over the next section. Then accordion-fold the rest of the booklet. Cut out the title box, and glue it on the section that ends up on top.
6. How Birds Fly Booklet: Cut out along the outer black line edges of the booklet. Fold so that the title is on the front. Crease along the edges of the cover, so that the wings appear to be "flying."
7. Preening, Molting, and Anting Booklet: Cut out along the outer black line edges of the circle. Note that there is a triangle in the middle, and it is a darker color than the rest of the booklet. Fold the "flaps" along the lines, so that the colored triangle is on the back, and the words are on the front. Tuck each flap under the one next to it. There is a diagram on the cut-out page. Also, see the pictures.
8. Bird Bath Booklet: Cut out along the outer black line edges of the booklet, keeping the "tubs" connected. Fold in the center, so that the title is on the front.
9. Types of Feathers Booklet: Cut out all of the pages of the booklet. Stack them together, with the title on the top. Then, punch a hole through all of the pages at the bottom of the ovals. Then, secure with a metal brad fastener. The pages will fan out like feathers, but keep them together for storing in the lapbook.

Flying Creatures of the Fifth Day
Lessons 1 - 6
Lapbook Student Instruction Guide

Decorate the outside/ cover of your lapbook. The cover of your lapbook has purposely been left blank so that your child may decorate it in any style he or she chooses. Your child may draw, paint, glue pictures, etc. You may print coloring sheets and glue them to the front. The ideas for the front cover are endless. Choose a topic or art project from this unit and HAVE FUN making it your own personalized lapbook!

Lesson 1:
o "What is Zoology?" Booklet: Do you know the definition of Zoology? It's a big word! Write the definition here.
o Animal Classification Booklet: Did you know that every animal (even you) is specifically named, according to classification? These classification names are pretty odd-sounding. Can you write the names here? How about a fun word search to help you remember the names? Also, answer the questions regarding definitions.
o How Do Birds Fly Booklet: I can't fly...can you?? Explain God's incredible design for birds to fly.
o Lesson 1 Vocabulary Booklet: Try your hand at these new words. If you don't know what they mean, look back through your lesson.

Lesson 2:
o Why People Need Birds Booklet: Do you think we need birds? We sure do. Explain why here.
o "Label the Bird" Booklet: Do you know all of the parts of a bird? They are different than our parts! Label the bird in the picture.
o "What Do Birds Have…" Booklet: Did you know that God made birds so special that they have something that NO other animal has??? What is it? Write it here.
o Bird Banter Booklet: Have you ever wondered how birds make such pretty songs? What is that sound that woodpeckers make? Here is the place to explore these sounds!
o Bird Banding Booklet: What is bird banding? Write about it here. You might want to draw a picture too.
o Audubon Booklet: Who was John James Audubon? Tell about him here.

Lesson 3:
o Types of Feathers Booklet: Did you know that there were many kinds of feathers? How many have you seen? Write about the different types here. You can also fan out this booklet to look like a "plume" of feathers!
o Lesson 3 Vocabulary Booklet: Have you learned these new words during your study? Define preening, molting, and anting.
o Label the Feather Booklet: What are the different parts of the feather called? Label this feather, and you may choose to color it also.
o Bird Baths Booklet: How do birds take a bath? Is it just like you? Explain the different ways here, and color the tub!

Lesson 4:
- Flying Booklet: Can you fly like a bird? How do birds glide, steer, and soar? Tell about this here.
- Migration Booklet: Do you know what it is to migrate? Why do birds migrate? Where do the birds go, and how do they know how to get there? Explain here.
- Arctic Tern Booklet: Have you ever seen a bird called an Arctic Tern? What is special about their migration?

Lesson 5:
- Types of Nests & Nesters Booklet: Have you ever seen a bird nest….up close? There are many different types. Tell about them here, and you may want to draw or glue pictures in also.
- Birds That Don't Build Nests Booklet: Did you know that there are birds who DON'T build nests? Write about these birds here.

Week 6:
- Copywork Booklet: Use your best penmanship to write this Old Testament verse. What do you think it means?
- Courtship Rituals Booklet: Each bird has its own way of "showing off" in order to have a mate. Can you name some of these ways?
- Label the Egg Booklet: Have you ever cracked open an egg and examined the parts? Try your hand at labeling this egg.
- Trivia Booklet: Now, se if you can answer these questions about interesting facts you have learned!

There are also 4 Amazing Facts Booklets. In these, you may write about anything you have learned. Are there some interesting facts you have learned? Take your pick, and write about them here. You may also want to draw or glue pictures inside these booklets.

Lessons 7 – 14 are covered in a separate lapbook.

Knowledge Box Central
www.knowledgeboxcentral.com
All materials copyrighted 2006
(Revised 2009)

Flying Creatures of the Fifth Day
Lessons 1 – 6 Lapbook
Teacher's Guide

Here, you'll find information to supplement your study. Jeannie Fulbright's book is so wonderfully filled with knowledge and wisdom. All of the information needed to complete all of the booklets can be found on the pages of her book. Below, I will tell you which pages hold specific "answers." Also, you'll find many other sites listed, where you may want to go for extra information, coloring pages, games, crafts, and ideas to extend your study.

Lesson 1:
o "What is Zoology?" Booklet: Answer found on page 1 of book.
o Animal Classification Booklet: Answers found on pages 2 – 5 of book.
o How Do Birds Fly Booklet: Answer found on pages 6 – 8 of book.
o Lesson 1 Vocabulary Booklet: Answers found on pages 12 – 17 of book.

Additional Resources for Lesson 1:

* "Classifying Critters" online game: http://www.hhmi.org/coolscience/critters/index.html
* "A to Z of Classification" - great online lesson:
http://web.archive.org/web/20040705153258/http:/education.leeds.ac.uk/~kh/technolo/ebp97/forest/azclass.htm
* Great site with lesson ideas for early learners: http://kindergartenclass.netfirms.com/mammals.htm

Lesson 2:
o Why People Need Birds Booklet: Do you think we need birds? We sure do. Explain why here.
o "Label the Bird" Booklet: Do you know all of the parts of a bird? They are different than our parts! Label the bird in the picture.
o "What Do Birds Have…" Booklet: Did you know that God made birds so special that they have something that NO other animal has??? What is it? Write it here.
o Bird Banter Booklet: Have you ever wondered how birds make such pretty songs? What is that sound that woodpeckers make? Here is the place to explore these sounds!
o Bird Banding Booklet: What is bird banding? Write about it here. You might want to draw a picture too.
o Audubon Booklet: Who was John James Audubon? Tell about him here.

Additional Resources for Lesson 2:
* "How Do Birds Learn To Sing?" - really neat website: http://www.cvco.org/science/audubon/songs.htm
* "How Birds Fly" online video: http://www.birdnote.org/birdnote.cfm?id=343 and http://www.birdnote.org/birdnote.cfm?id=344
* "Bird Banter" information: http://birding.about.com/gi/dynamic/offsite.htm?zi=1/XJ/Ya&sdn=birding&cdn=hobbies&tm=4&gps=44_9_950_505&f=20&su=p445.92.150.ip_&tt=14&bt=0&bts=0&zu=http%3A//www.inhs.uiuc.edu/chf/pub/virtualbird/student/les6.html
* WONDERFUL site! Listen to the songs of specific birds: http://birding.about.com/gi/dynamic/offsite.htm?zi=1/XJ/Ya&sdn=birding&cdn=hobbies&tm=202&gps=45_10_950_505&f=20&su=p445.92.150.ip_&tt=14&bt=0&bts=0&zu=http%3A//www.1000plus.com/BirdSong/birdsngb.html
* John James Audubon Society website – tons of resources here: http://www.audubon.org/bird/BoA/BOA_index.html
* Bird Banding: http://www.kidwings.com/teacher/birdbands/index.htm
* Bird Flight: http://www.nhm.org/birds/guide/pg018.html

Lesson 3:
o	Types of Feathers Booklet: Answers found on pages 41- 49
o	Lesson 3 Vocabulary Booklet: Answers found on pages 42 - 53
o	Label the Feather Booklet: Answers found on page 43
o	Bird Baths Booklet: Answerss found on pages 52 - 53

Additional Resources for Lesson 3:
*	Types of Feathers: http://www.peteducation.com/article.cfm?cls=15&cat=1829&articleid=2776
*	Another site on types of feathers (ignore the part about bird feathers "evolving" from reptile scales – and the rest is good information!): http://birds.ecoport.org/Identification/EBfeathers-type.htm
*	Bird Bathing: http://www.birdwatchireland.ie/working_with_birds/pages/18.html
*	Bathing and Preening: http://www.garden-birds.co.uk/information/bathing.htm

Lesson 4:
o	Flying Booklet: Answers found on Pages 57 - 60
o	Migration Booklet: Answers found on pages 61 - 68
o	Arctic Tern Booklet: Answers found on page 67

Additional Resources for Lesson 4:
*	Great site about migration: http://www.learner.org/jnorth/
*	Migration Game Online: http://www.on.ec.gc.ca/greatlakeskids/migration/migration.html
*	Arctic Tern: http://library.thinkquest.org/3500/arctic_tern.html

Lesson 5:
o	Types of Nests & Nesters Booklet: Answers found on pages 73 - 84
o	Birds That Don't Build Nests Booklet: Answers found on page 76 – 78

Additional Resources for Lesson 5:
*	Building a Bird Box (online tutorial): http://www.highlightskids.com/Magazine/May06/h1magazineFlashObjects/bluebirdBox.asp
*	Great pictures of bird nests: http://www.kidwings.com/nests/main.htm

Week 6:
o	Copywork Booklet
o	Courtship Rituals Booklet: Answers found on page 89 - 92
o	Label the Egg Booklet: Answers found on page 94
o	Trivia Booklet: Answers thoughout the chapter

Additional Resources for Lesson 6:
*	Bird Courtship Rituals: http://ladywildlife.com/animal/birdcourtship.html
*	Baby Bird Hatchling Craft: http://www.runnerduck.com/kc_baby_bird_egg.htm

Additional Resources:

* Bird Coloring Pages: http://www.cvco.org/science/audubon/coloring.htm
*
* Tons of "bird stuff:" http://www.cvco.org/science/audubon/KIDSCORN.htm

* Everything about Hummingbirds: http://www.hummingbirdworld.com/h/
* Bird Trivia site: http://www.wbu.com/chipperwoods/kids.htm
* TONS of info about birds: http://www.kidskonnect.com/Birds/BirdsHome.html
* Colorful pictures of birds, and a quiz: http://www.english-zone.com/vocab/birds/birdies.html
* John James Audubon Society – TONS of resources here: http://www.audubon.org/bird/BoA/BOA_index.html
* Bluebird "Growing Up" Game – SO CUTE! : http://www.sialis.org/bluebirdgrowingupgame.htm

* How to draw a bird (instruction): http://www.billybear4kids.com/Learn2Draw/sheets/BlueBird.html
* Origami Bird: http://www.yasutomo.com/project/bluebird.htm
* Bird Cross-Stitch Patterns: http://www.birdcrossstitch.com/
* Old Legend "How the Bluebird and Coyote Got Their Colors" story: http://www.sialis.org/bluebirdstory.htm
* Bird Cam: http://www.beakspeak.com/birdcams/
* Bird Matching Game: http://www.kidwings.com/games/matchinggame/birds/index.htm
* Bird Slider Puzzle: http://www.kidwings.com/games/sliderpuzzle/snowyegret/index.html
* BIRDO Bingo Game: http://www.kidwings.com/teacher/birdo/index.htm
* General Info on Birds: http://www.biokids.umich.edu/critters/Aves
* Lots of Bird Crafts: http://www.dltk-kids.com/animals/birds.html
* More Bird Crafts: http://www.daniellesplace.com/html/birdcrafts.html

**** Check our site for "Bird-Related" CopyWork!! www.knowledgeboxcentral.com

Types of Nests & Nesters

Bowers

Weavers

No Nesters

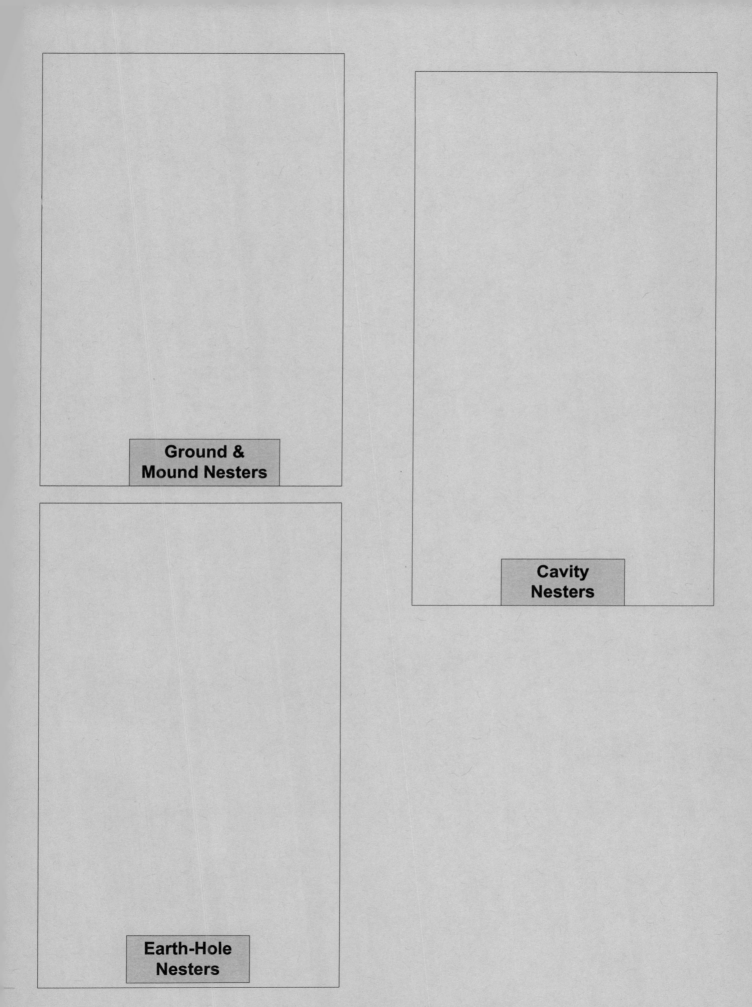

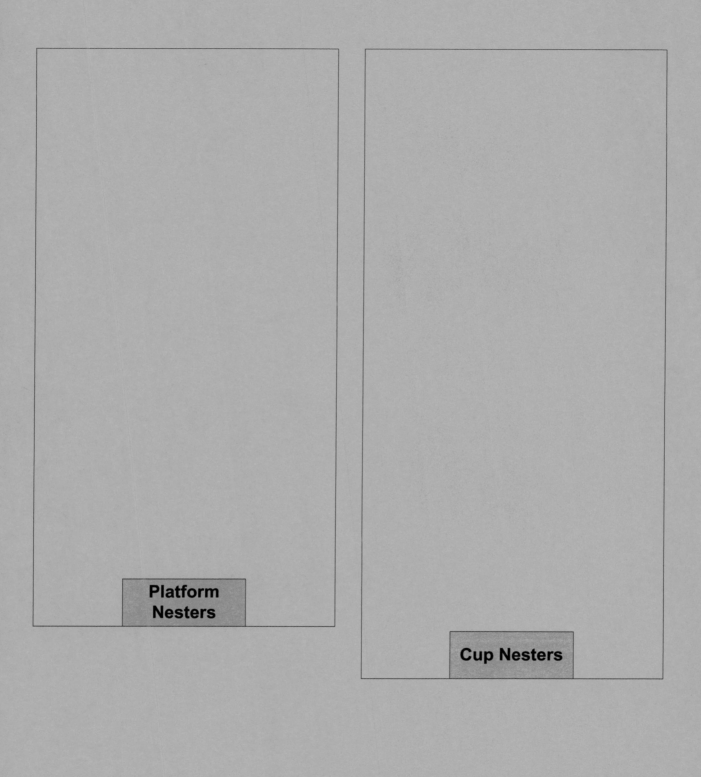

Adherant Nests

Bird Banter

How does a bird make sound?

What is a bird "call?"

What is a bird "song?"

What is the purpose of a bird call?	What is "drumming?"
Other ways birds communicate:	

Label the parts of the bird.

Forehead
Crown
Nape
Back
Wing
Rump
Tail
Upper Mandible
Lower mandible
Chin
Throat
Breast
Belly
Flank
Tarsus

Lesson 1 Vocabulary

Habitat

Instinct

Extinction

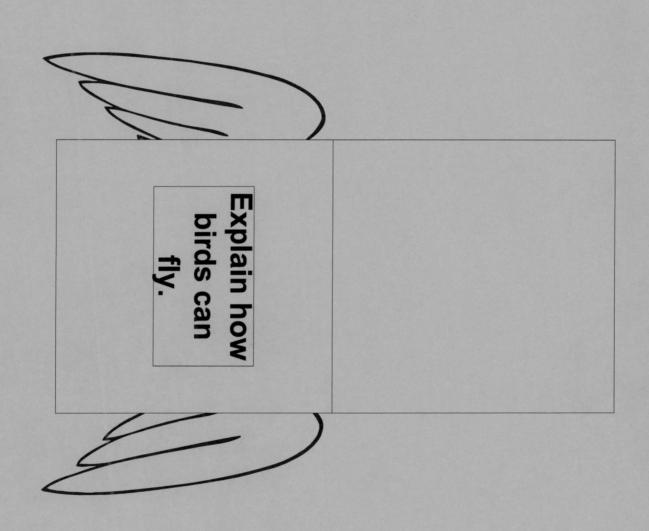

Explain how birds can fly.

Animal Classification

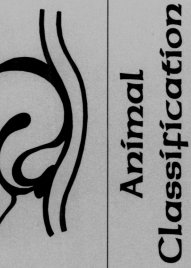

Define "vertebrate"
_____
_____
_____

Define "invertebrate"
_____
_____
_____

Scientists who study animals are called

_____

The process of grouping and naming all living things is called:

_____

Can you name the order of the classification system?
Try to write the names in order here:

_____
_____
_____
_____
_____
_____
_____

Why are many of the classification groups written in Latin?

_____
_____
_____
_____

Animal Classification Word Search – Words may be found in any direction, including backwards and diagonal.

SPECIES   ORDER   GENUS   KINGDOM
FAMILY   PHYLUM   CLASS

```
A N M L M O D G N I K S M
S Y D E H U C E E Y C O R U H
I L I G Y O O N K D L D N C S O
N I Y U S S M S D G O D N A A
L M N S U P U U N G E F S N H
P A N N S P E I Y C L G D U A
H F E E R O K C G E E M A I Y
Y G O R D E R U I O K L E N O
L E R M P U H L I E L H I S S
U G M S I C Y C F I S S Y C S M
M D E C O R E S U M H L D A N
H E L P L P Y P S F D L R
C N L E S A S G R K Y N A C P
R P L N E S S Y I F A M I N O
E L E D N M E M U S S D C S I
```

What is *binomial nomenclature*?

_____
_____
_____

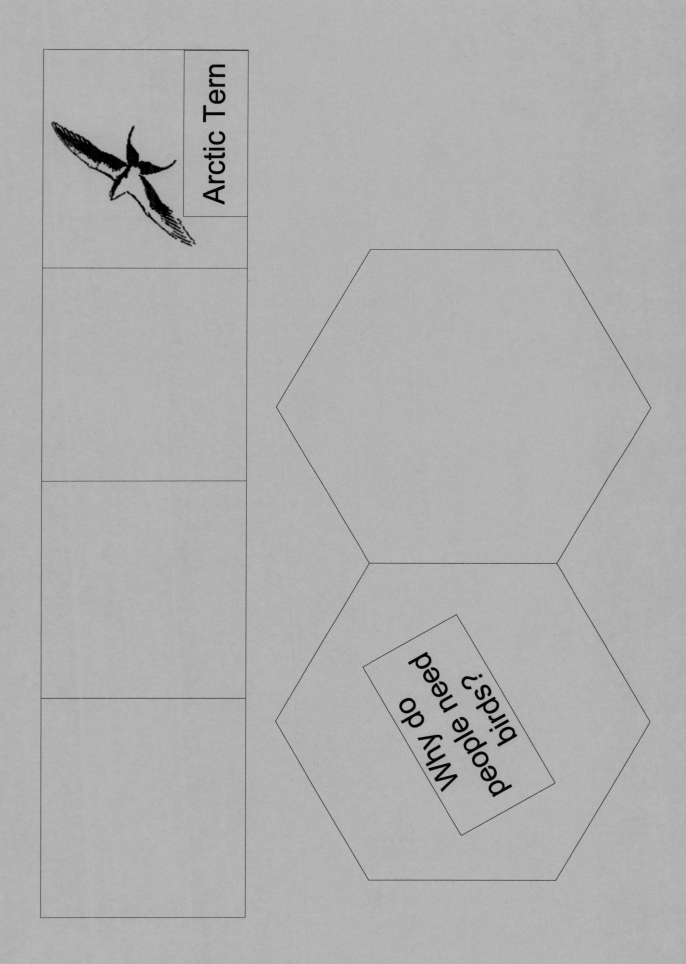

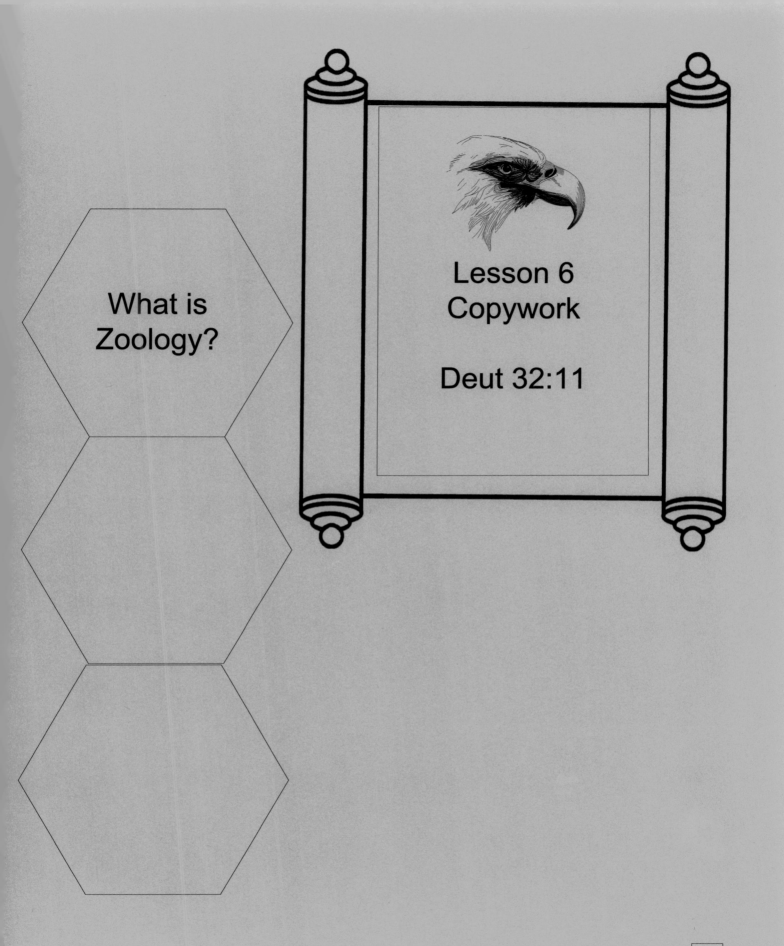

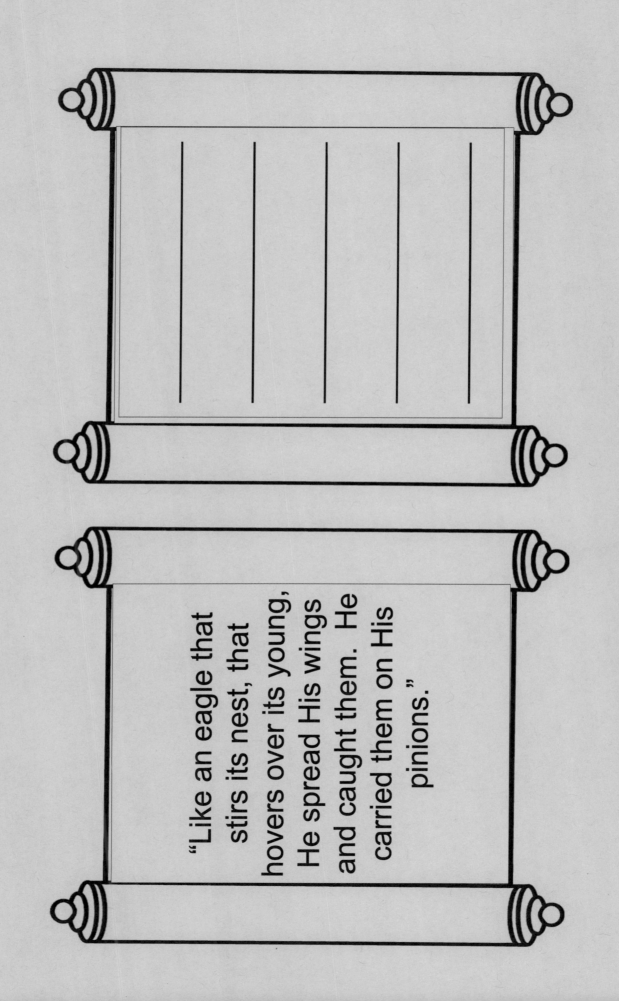

Migration

Why do birds migrate?

Where to go?

Landmarks

Sun & Stars

Magnetic Fields

Eating

Dangers

How High

What does a bird have, that NO OTHER animal type has?

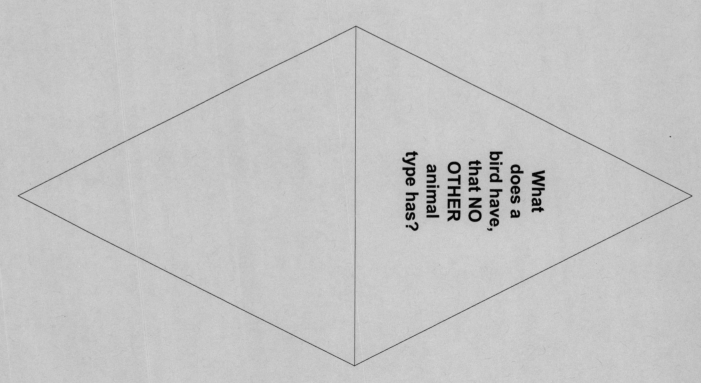

Amazing Fact

Amazing Fact

Amazing Fact

Amazing FAct

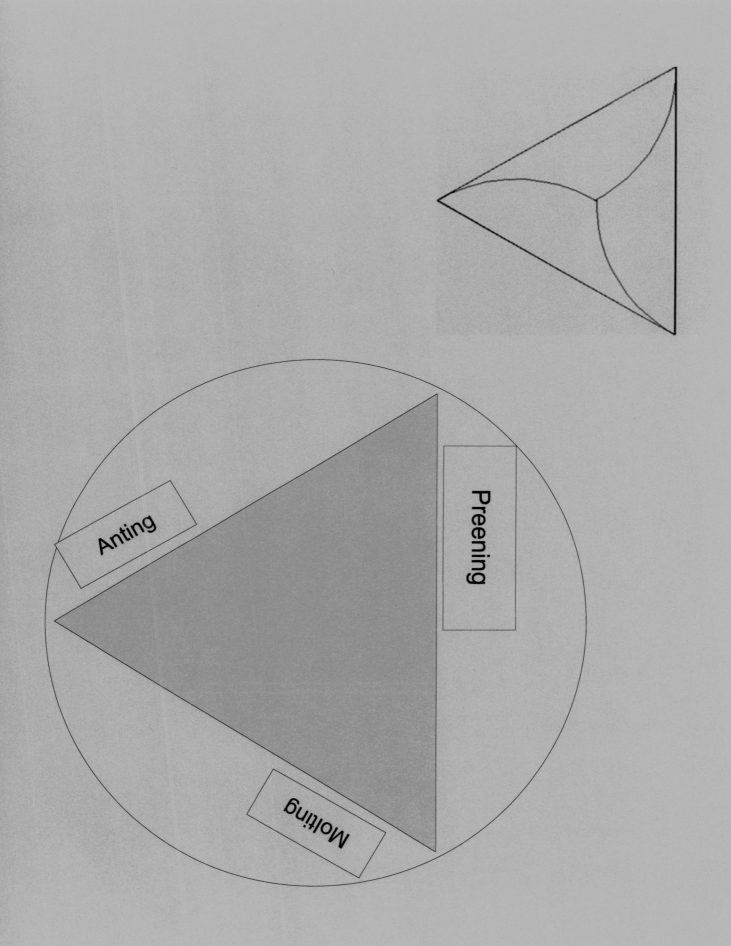

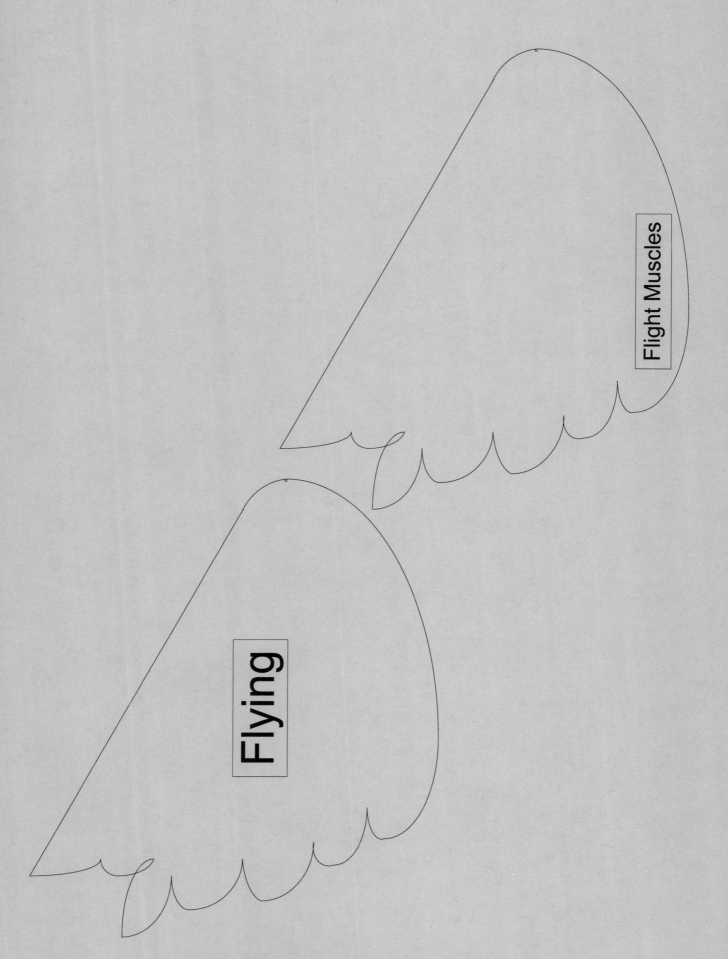

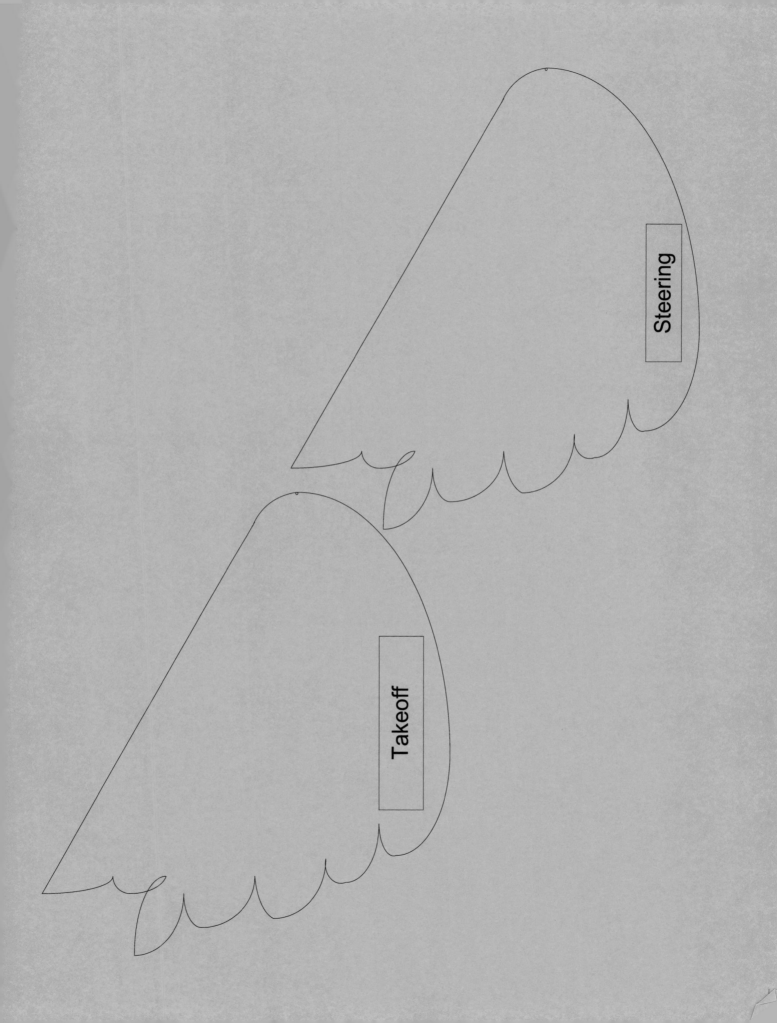

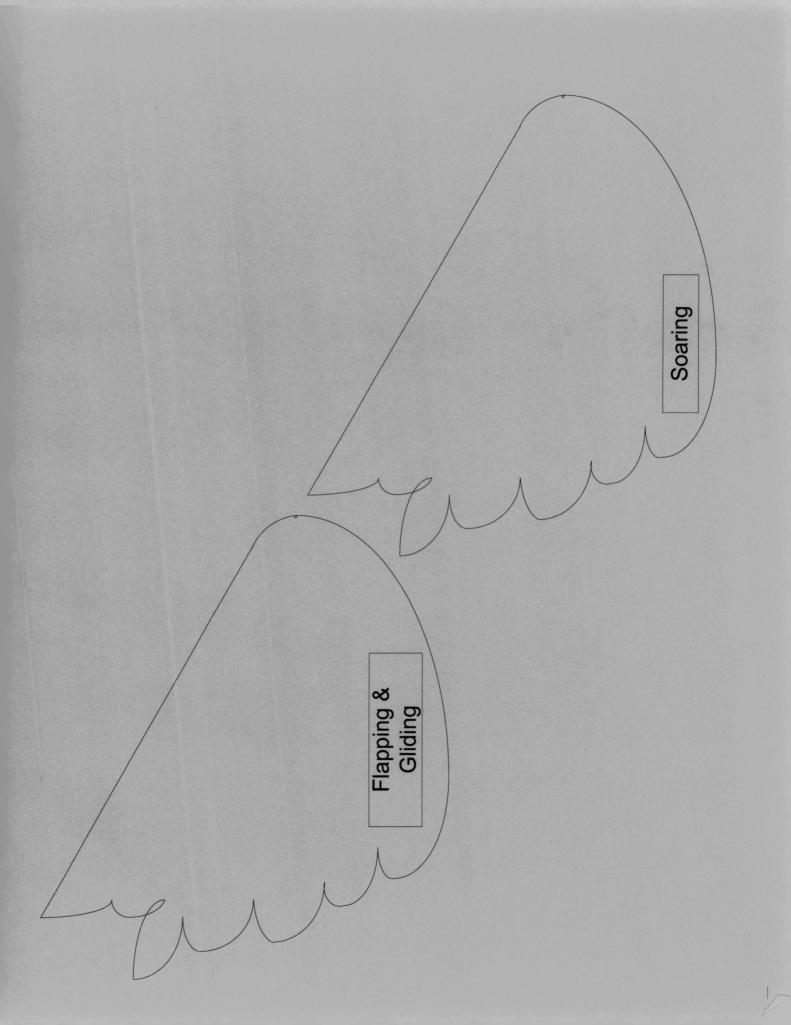

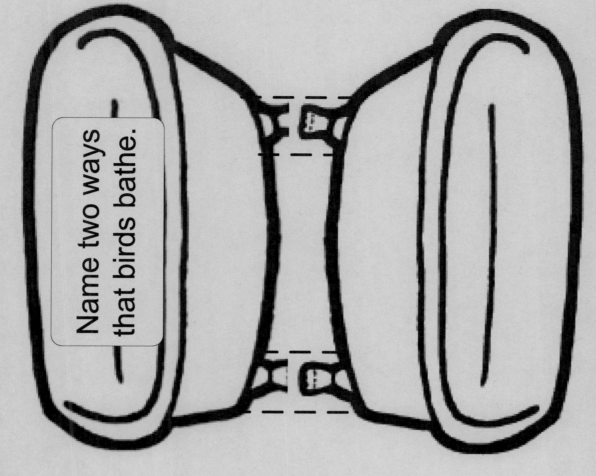

Name two ways that birds bathe.

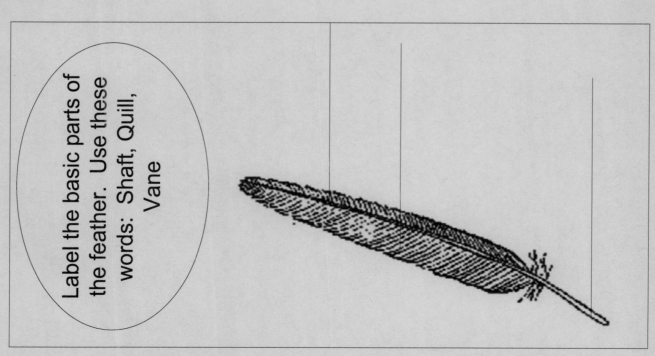

Label the basic parts of the feather. Use these words: Shaft, Quill, Vane

Lesson 6 Trivia

Which is more colorful, a male or a female bird?

What do you call a group of eggs in a nest?

What is it called when a mother bird sits on her eggs?

What is the name of the bump on the bird's beak that helps it break out of the shell?

If a bird is completely dependent on its parents, what is it called?

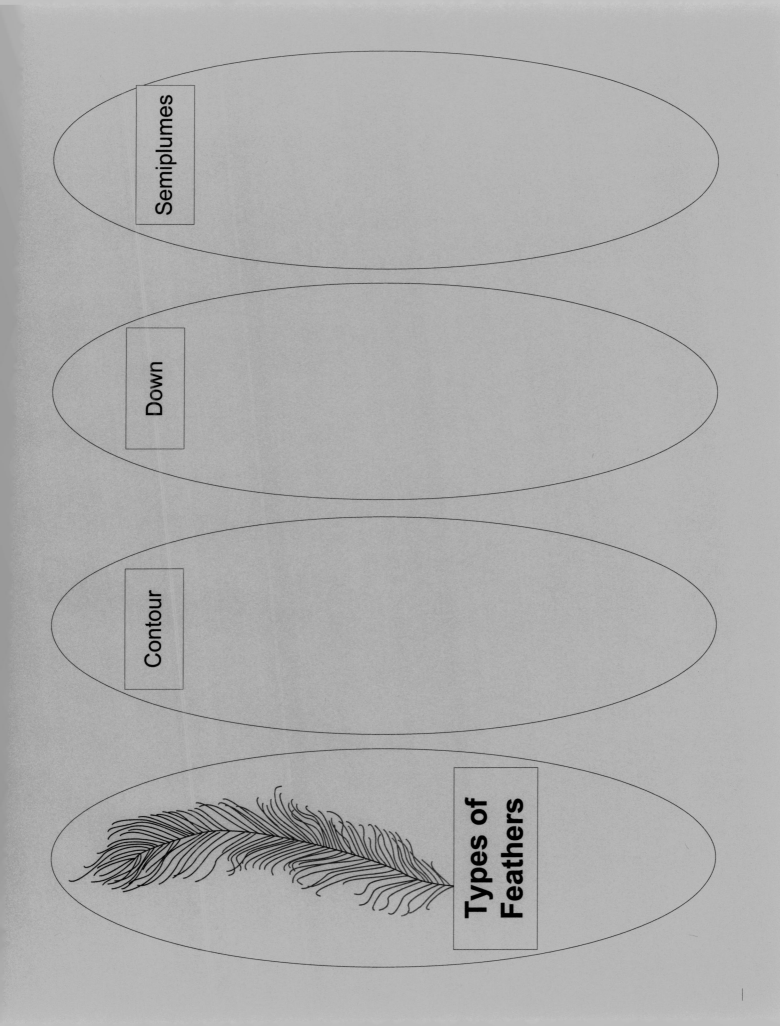

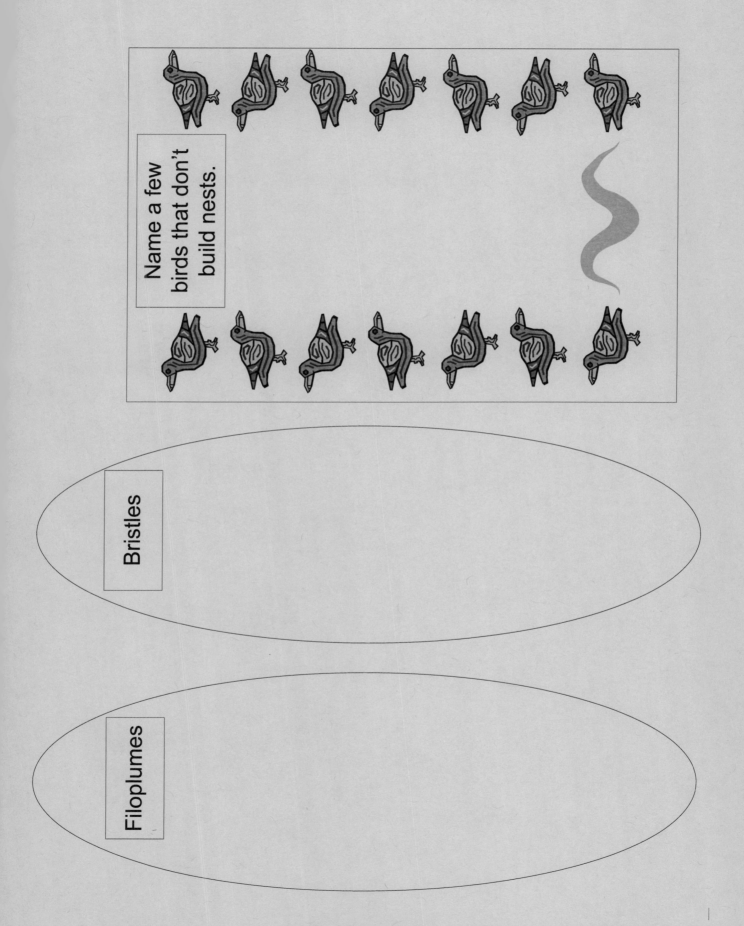

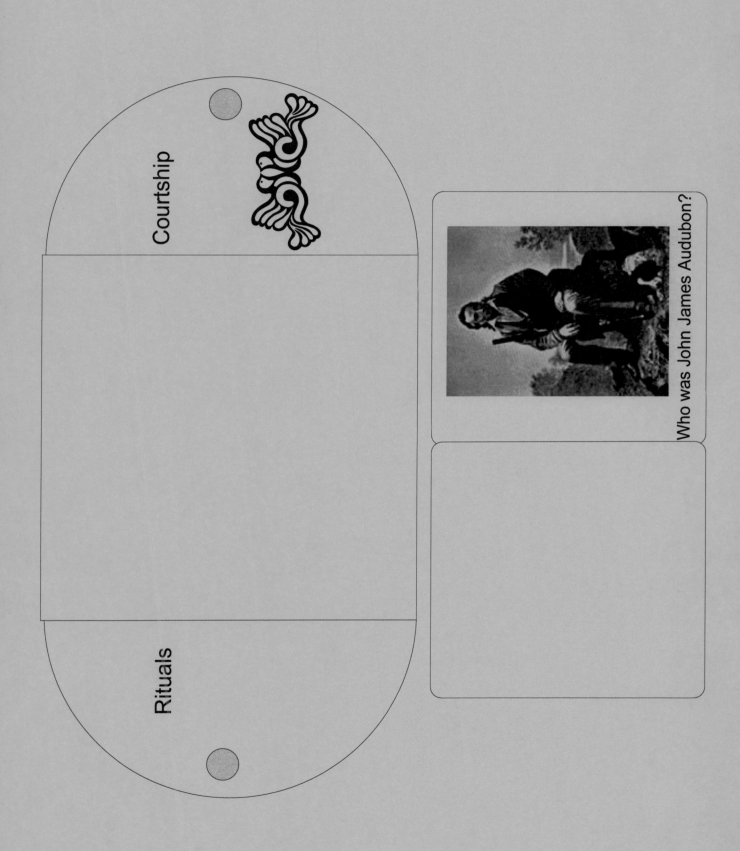

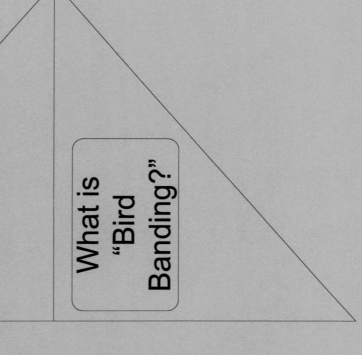

What is "Bird Banding?"

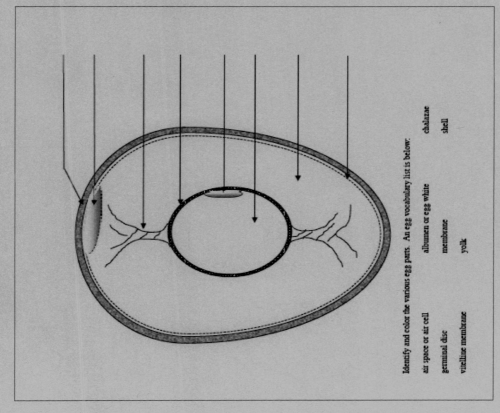

Identify and color the various egg parts. An egg vocabulary list is below:

air space or air cell   albumen or egg white   chalazae
germinal disc   membrane   shell
vitelline membrane   yolk

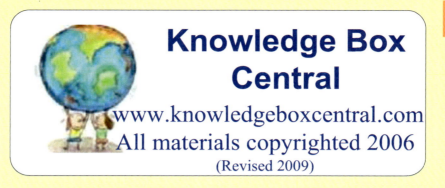

L_FCFD2_D

Welcome to our "Exploring Creation With Zoology 1: Flying Creatures of the Fifth Day" Lapbook (Lessons 7-14)

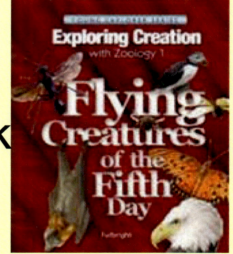

Designed by Dr. Cyndi Kinney with expressed permission from Apologia Science and Jeannie Fulbright

This is the "Pre-Printed Do-It-Yourself" format of this product.

The templates have been printed on paper that is colored specifically to improve information retention, as determined by scientific research.

Exploring Creation with Zoology 1: *Flying Creatures of the Fifth Day* (Lessons 7-14) Lapbook. This lapbook has been specifically designed for use with the book, by Jeannie Fulbright and Apologia Science.

This lapbook covers Lessons 7-14, and lessons 1-6 are covered in a separate lapbook.

"Exploring Creation With Zoology 1: Flying Creatures of the Fifth Day" Lapbook for Lessons 7-14

Published by:

Knowledge Box Central
155 Clements Rd.
Plain Dealing, La. 71064

All information and graphics within this product are originals or have been used with permission from its owners, and credit has been given when appropriate. These include, but are not limited to the following: www.iclipart.com, and Art Explosion Clipart.

All rights reserved. No part of this book may be reproduced or transmitted in any form or by any means, electronic or mechanical, including photocopying, recording or by any information storage and retrieval system without written permission from the author. The Ebook and Cd Rom Formats are licensed for use by ONLY the household family of the purchaser of the product, allowing for copies to be made for each child within THAT household ONLY. "Pre-Printed/Do-It-Yourself" formats may NOT be copied. These are meant to be used for 1 student ONLY. "Pre-Assembled" formats may NOT be copied in any way and are also meant to be used for 1 student ONLY. Any violation of this policy is also a violation of the United States Copyright Laws.

If you have any questions regarding this copyright/licensure agreement, please contact cyndi@knowledgeboxcentral.com.

Copyright © 2009 Knowledge Box Central

www.knowledgeboxcentral.com

Printed in the United States of America

PLEASE NOTE: This is the second of 2 lapbooks for this book, "Exploring Creation With Zoology 1: Flying Creatures of the Fifth Day."

This particular lapbook ONLY covers Lessons 7 through 14.
You will need BOTH lapbooks in order to complete the entire book in lapbook format.

How do I get started?

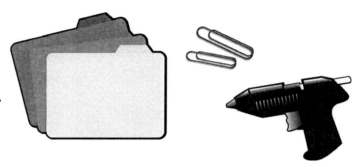

First, you will want to gather your supplies.

*** Assembly:

   *Folders: We use colored file folders, which can be found at Walmart, Sam's, Office Depot, Costco, etc. You will need between 2 and 4 file folders, depending on which product you have purchased. You may use manilla folders if you prefer, but we have found that children respond better with the brightly colored folders. Don't worry about the tabs….they aren't important. ***If you prefer, you can purchase the assembled lapbook bases from our website.***

   *Glue: For the folder assembly, we use hot glue. For booklet assembly, we use glue sticks and sometimes hot glue, depending on the specific booklet. We have found that bottle glue stays wet for too long, so it's not a great choice for lapbooking.

   *Other Supplies: Of course, you will need scissors. Many booklets require additional supplies. Some of these include metal brad fasteners, paper clips, ribbon, yarn, staples, hole puncher, etc. You may want to add decorations of your own, including stickers, buttons, coloring pages, cut-out clipart, etc. The most important thing is to use your imagination! Make it your own!!

Ok. I've gathered the supplies. Now how do I use this product?

Inside, you will find several sections. They are as follows:

1. **Lapbook Assembly Guide:** This section is written directly to the student, in language that he or she can understand. However, depending on the age of the child, there may be some parent/teacher assistance needed. These instructions will tell the student exactly how to assemble the lapbook base and how to cut out and assemble each booklet. Here, they will find a layout of where each booklet should be placed in the lapbook and pictures of a completed lapbook. They will also tell the student exactly what should be written inside each booklet as he or she comes to it during the study.

2. **Teacher's Guide**: This section is a great resource for the parent/teacher. In this section, you will find the page number where each answer may be found in the book. You will also find suggestions of extra activities that you may want to use with your student.

3. **Templates:** This section includes ALL of the templates for the booklets. These have been printed on colors that will help to improve retention of the information presented, according to scientific research on color psychology.

Exploring Creation With Zoology 1:
Flying Creatures of the Fifth Day Lessons 7-14
Lapbook Assembly Guide

You will need 3 folders of any color. Take each one and fold both sides toward the original middle fold and make firm creases on these folds (Figure 1). Then glue (and staple if needed) the backs of the small flaps together (Figure 2).

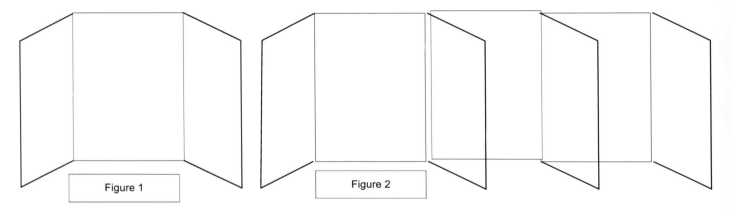

This is the "Layout" for your lapbook. The shapes are not exact on the layout, but you will get the idea of where each booklet should go inside your lapbook.

Inside of 1st Folder:

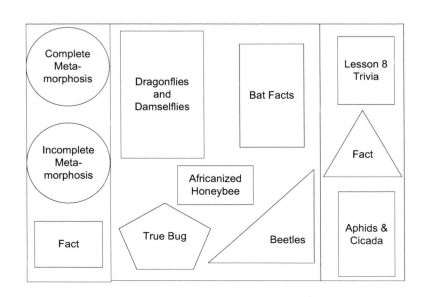

Inside of 2nd Folder:

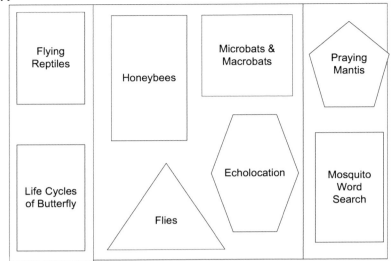

Inside of 3rd Folder:

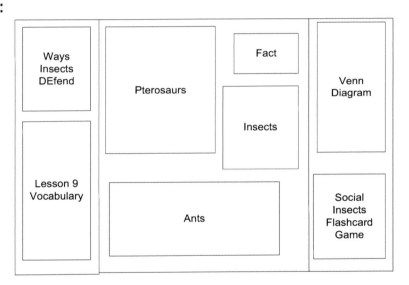

Outside of 3rd Folder:

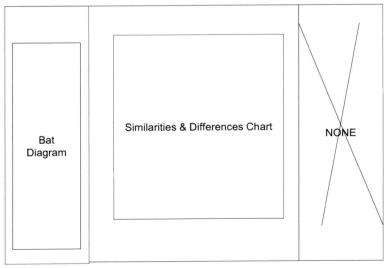

We have added pictures of a completed lapbook!!! This should help in figuring out how to assemble the booklets and then how to put it all together!

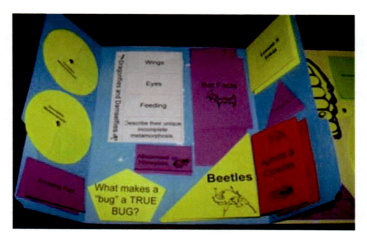

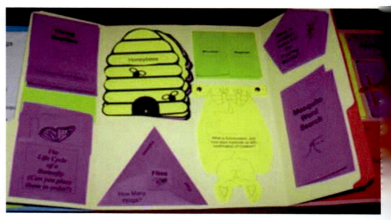

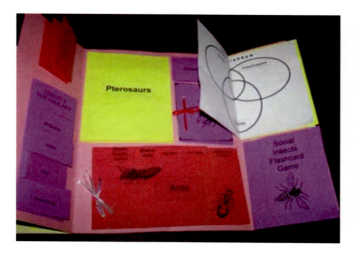

Knowledge Box Central
www.knowledgeboxcentral.com
All materials copyrighted 2006
(Revised 2009)

Flying Creatures of the Fifth Day
Lessons 7 - 14
Lapbook Assembly Guide

Inside of 1st Folder:

1. Complete Metamorphosis Booklet: Cut out both circles. Then cut out the wedge from the circle with the title on it. Stack them, with the title on top. Punch a hole through the center, and secure together with a metal brad fastener.
2. Incomplete Metamorphosis Booklet: Cut out both circles. Then cut out the wedge from the circle with the title on it. Stack them, with the title on top. Punch a hole through the center, and secure together with a metal brad fastener.
3. Dragonflies and Damselflies Booklet: Cut out along the outer black line edges of the booklet and the text boxes. Then, fold along the vertical line that is near the center, so that the title, "Dragonflies and Damselflies) is still visible on the edge. Glue the text boxes onto the side of the booklet that the title folds over. Now cut along the lines between the words (Wings, Eyes, Feeding, and Describe their incomplete metamorphosis), creating "flaps," under which you will write your descriptions.
4. Africanized Honeybee Booklet: Cut out along the outer black line edges. Then, fold along the center line so that the title is on the front.
5. Bats Booklet: Cut out along the outer black line edges of the booklet and text boxes. Tri-fold the booklet, so that the title is on the front. Now glue each title box onto a page within the booklet.
6. True Bug Booklet: Cut out along the outer black line edges, and then fold along the center line so that the title and graphic are on the front.
7. Beetles Booklet: Cut out along the outer black line edges of the booklet. Then fold each corner in toward the middle, so that all 4 points meet in the center, with the words and graphics showing. Now, fold the booklet diagonally, so that all of the words and other folds are now on the inside. Cut out the title label, and glue it to the outside. Cut out the "Beneficial or Pesky" label, and glue it in the center of the inside (under the points that come together in the center). See pictures for a better idea of what this will look like.
8. Aphids & Cicadas Booklet: Cut out along the outer black line edges. Then accordion-fold the booklet so that the title is on the front and a blank is on the back.
9. Amazing Facts (2) Booklets: Cut out along the outer black line edges of these booklets, and fold along the center lines so that the titles are on the front.
10. Lesson 8 Trivia Booklet: Cut out along the outer black line edges of this "L" shape. Then, fold the lower right side of the "L" over on top of the square to its left. Now you have an "I" shaped booklet. Accordion-fold so that the title is on the top.

Inside of 2nd t Folder:

1. Flying Reptiles Booklet: Cut out along the outer black line edges of each page. Then, stack them on top of each other, with the title on top and each page being a little longer than the one before. Now staple at the top of the stack to hold them together.

2. Life Cycle of a Butterfly Booklet: Cut out along the outer black line edges of each rectangle (each one has a different portion of the life cycle on it) and also along the outer black line edges of the "pocket" with the title on it. Now fold the "pocket" along the horizontal line, and glue the edges, so that it creates a "pocket" for the life cycle "cards." Look at the picture of the completed lapbook, and you will get a better idea of how this w look.

3. Honeybees Booklet: Cut out along the outer black line edges of each page. Then, stack them together, with the title on top. Punch a hole through the "door" to the hive, and secure with a metal fastener brad.

4. Microbats & Macrobats Booklet: Cut out along the outer black line edges. Than, fold along the horizontal line, so that the words are on the outside. Now, cut along the line that runs between the 2 words, but only up to the fold.

5. Bat Echolocation Booklet: Cut out along the outer black line edges of each page. Stack together, with the title on top and the verse and blank pages following. Punch 2 holes along the top, and secure with ribbon or metal brad fasteners. Remember, bats hang upside down, so this booklet will be "upside down."

6. Flies Booklet: Cut out along the outer black line edges of the booklet. Fold each curved side in toward the middle, so that the words end up on the outside. Cut out the "Flies" label. Glue the label on one corner, and secure it to ONLY one curved edge. Fold according to the small diagram on that page, and the "Flies" label will be in front. See the picture of the completed lapbook for a better idea of how this will look.

7. Praying Mantis Booklet: Cut out along the outer black line edges , and fold along the center line so that the title is on the front.

8. Mosquito Word Search Booklet: Cut out along the outer black line edges , and fold in the center, vertically, so that the title is on the front.

Inside of 3rd Folder:

1. "Ways insects defend…" Booklet: Cut out along the outer black line edges of the booklet. Fold accordion-style, so that the title is on the front.

2. Lesson 9 Vocabulary Booklet: Cut out along the outer black line edges. Then fold along the center vertical line, so that the words are all on the outside. Now, cut along the lines between the vocabulary words, so that you create "flaps."

3. Amazing Fact Booklet: Cut out along the outer black line edges. Then, fold along the center line so that the title is on the front.

4. Pterosaurs Booklet: Cut out along the outer black line edges of the large booklet. Cut out the title box. Fold the large booklet in the center, vertically, so that the word is on the inside. Now, glue the title box in the center on the outside. Cut out the 4 smaller booklets, and fold along their center horizontal lines so that their titles are on the front. Now, glue all 4 of these small booklets inside the large booklet….2 on each side.

5. Insects Booklet: Cut out along the outer black line edges of each page. Stack them on top of each other, with the title on the top. Punch 2 holes along the left side. Secure with a ribbon.

6. Venn Diagram Booklet: Cut out along the outer black line edges of the booklet. Then, fold along its middle, vertically. Now, glue this boklet to a slightly larger piece of paper of a different color, creating a border.

7. Ants Booklet: Cut out along the outer black line edges of the each page. Stack them together, so that the title is on the front and each page's tab gets progressively longer. Now punch 2 holes in the left side, and secure with a ribbon or metal fastener brads.

8. Social Insects Flashcard Game Booklet: Cut out along the outer black line edges of the the booklet. Now, fold along both vertical lines, so that you create a "flap" on both ends. Now, glue these "flaps" down on the edges, which creates pockets. Now cut out the "flashcards," and put them in the pockets you have just created.

Outside of 3rd Folder:

1. Label the Bat Booklet: Cut out along the outer black line edges. Glue to a slightly larger piece of paper of a different color, creating a small border.

2. Similarities & Differences Booklet: Cut out along the outer black line edges. Glue to a slightly larger piece of paper of a different color, creating a small border.

Knowledge Box Central

www.knowledgeboxcentral.com
All materials copyrighted 2006

Flying Creatures of the Fifth Day
Lessons 7 – 14 Lapbook
Student Instruction Guide

Decorate the outside/ cover of your lapbook. The cover of your lapbook has purposely been left blank so that your child may decorate it in any style he or she chooses. Your child may draw, paint, glue pictures, etc. You may print coloring sheets suggested on the *Tapestry of Grace* web site and glue them to the front. The ideas for the front cover are endless. Choose a topic or art project from this unit and HAVE FUN making it your own personalized lapbook!

Lesson 7:
o	Microbats & Macrobats Booklet: Have you ever seen a bat? Was it a microbat or a macrobat? What are the differences? Write about them here. You may also want to draw or glue ictures.
o	Echolocation Booklet: Can bats hear? What is their special type of hearing, and how does it confirm creation? Answer these questions here.
o	Bat Facts Booklet: Bats are very interesting creatures. See if you can answer these questions about their unique characteristics.
o	Bat Anatomy Booklet: Do you know all of the parts of a bat? Did you know they even have thumbs??? Label this bat.

Lesson 8:
o	Flying Reptiles Booklet: Have you ever seen a flying reptile? Did you even know that there was suck a thing? What does the Bible say about them? Explain here...and draw pictures if you like!
o	Pterosaurs Booklet: God made 2 different types of Pterosaurs. Can you tell about them here?
o	Lesson 8 Trivia Booklet: See if you can remember these interesting facts about flying reptiles.

Lesson 9:
o	Insects Booklet: Do you like insects? What are you favorite kinds? Have you ever noticed how amazing God made their eyes? Tell about these incredible creatures in this booklet. Draw pictures if you like!
o	Vocabulary Booklet: Have you learned these new words during your study? Define ovipositor, clasp, cerci, and entomology here.

Lesson 10:
o	Complete and Incomplete Metamorphosis Booklets: Try to say this big word: metamorphosis. That's a hard word to say! Do you know what it means? Turn the wheels, and write the stages of each. What is different?
o	"How Insects Defend" Booklet: Did you know that insects can defend and protect themselves...even though they are very small? How do they do this? Explain it here.

Lesson 11:
o	Ants Booklet: Wow...ants are amazing! Have you ever watched them work? How do they do it?? Write about the different types of ants here. You may draw or glue pictures on the pages also.
o	Honeybees Booklet: Do you like honey? Where does it come from? Tell about the honeybees here.
o	Africanized Honeybee Booklet: What's so different about this type of bee? Where are they found? Tell about them here.
o	Social Insects Flashcard Trivia Booklet: What does it mean to be a "social" insect? Which insects are considered to be "social?" See if you can answer these questions about these particular types of insects.

Lesson 12:
- Beetles Booklets: Have you ever seen a colorful beetle? Isn't it amazing how God made them? Are they pests...or are they useful? See if you can tell about them here.
- Flies Booklet: Have you ever been nagged by flies at a picnic? Why are they important to us? Explain what you know about them here.
- Mosquito Word Search Booklet: Mosquitoes are really pesky insects. Do you have them at your house? See if you can find all of this "mosquito words" in the puzzle.
- True Bug Booklet: Do you call everything that buzzes around a "bug?" How do you know if it's really a bug? Is a butterfly a bug? How about a spider? What about a wasp? See if you can figure out how to tell a true bug from the others.

Lesson 13:
- Praying Mantis Booklet: Have you ever seen a Praying Mantis? Where did it get its name? Explain this unique insect.
- Dragonflies & Damselflies Booklet: Have you ever seen dragonflies and damselflies? Do you know how they are different? Explain it here.
- Venn Diagram Booklet: There are many similarities and differences between crickets, grasshoppers, and katydids. Use this venn diagram to explore these.
- Aphids and Cicadas Booklet: What is similar and different between these? Hoe does a cicada confirm creation? Explain these here.

Lesson 14:
- Life Cycle of a Butterfly Booklet: Aren't butterflies just beautiful? Do they start out looking ANYTHING like a butterfly? Try to put these stages of the butterfly's life cycle in order.
- Butterfly, Moth, Skipper Chart (Differences & Similarities) Booklet: What are the differences between butterflies, moths, and skippers? Sometimes they look the same, don't they? Try to complete this chart about how similar and different they really are.

There are also 3 Amazing Facts Booklets. In these, you may write about anything you have learned. Are there some interesting facts you have learned? Take your pick, and write about them here. You may also want to draw or glue pictures inside these booklets.

Lessons 1 – 6 are covered in a separate lapbook.

Knowledge Box Central
www.knowledgeboxcentral.com
All materials copyrighted 2006
(Revised 2009)

Flying Creatures of the Fifth Day
Lessons 7 – 14 Lapbook
Teacher's Guide

Here, you'll find information to supplement your study. Jeannie Fulbright's book is so wonderfully filled with knowledge and wisdom. All of the information needed to complete all of the booklets can be found on the pages of her book. Below, I will tell you which pages hold specific "answers." Also, you'll find many other sites listed, where you may want to go for extra information, coloring pages, games, crafts, and ideas to extend your study.

Lesson 7:
- Microbats & Macrobats Booklet: Answers found on pages 108 - 111
- Echolocation Booklet: Answers found on pages 106 - 107
- Bat Facts Booklet: Answers found throughout this chapter
- Bat Anatomy Booklet: Answers found on pages 104 - 105

Additional Resources for Lesson 7:

* Several sites about bats:
http://members.aol.com/bats4kids/index.htm
http://www.kidzone.ws/animals/bats/
http://www.batworld.org/kids_page/kids_page.html
http://art-smart.ci.manchester.ct.us/easy-bat/easy-bat.html

Lesson 8:
- Flying Reptiles Booklet: Answers found on pages 119 - 123
- Pterosaurs Booklet: Answers found on pages 123 - 127
- Lesson 8 Trivia Booklet: Answers found throughout the chapter.

Additional Resources for Lesson 8:
**Be careful on the internet with this chapter….many sites confuse these with dinosaurs.
* Pterosaur Coloring Page: http://homeschooling.about.com/od/freeprintables/ss/dinosaurprint_6.htm
* Pterosaur Coloring Page: http://www.dibujosparapintar.com/english_activities/dr_dinosaurs.html#
* Pteranodon Coloring Page: http://www.daniellesplace.com/html/dinosaurs.html

Lesson 9:
- Insects Booklet: Answers found throughout this chapter
- Vocabulary Booklet: Answers fond throughout this chapter

Additional Resources for Lesson 9:

* Insect Life Cycle diagram: http://www.kidfish.bc.ca/cycle.htm
* LOTS of insect information: http://www.earthlife.net/insects/six.html
* Insect coloring pages: http://www.coloring.ws/insect.htm
* This site is FULL of insect "stuff" : http://www.ivyhall.district96.k12.il.us/4th/kkhp/1insects/bugmenu.html

Lesson 10:
- Complete and Incomplete Metamorphosis Booklets: Answers found on pages 149 - 154
- "How Insects Defend" Booklet: Answers found on pages 154 - 160

Additional Resources for Lesson 10:
* Metamorphosis information: http://www.bijlmakers.com/entomology/begin.htm
* How insects defend themselves: http://www.sidney.ars.usda.gov/sidebar/justforkids2.html

Lesson 11:
- Ants Booklet: Answers found on pages 163 - 169
- Honeybees Booklet: Answers found on pages 169 - 173
- Africanized Honeybee Booklet: Answers found on pages 176 - 177
- Social Insects Flashcard Trivia Booklet: Answers found throughout chapter

Additional Resources for Lesson 11:
* Ants Bible Lesson: http://www.daniellesplace.com/html/freeantlesson.html
* Really nice site about ants: http://home.att.net/~B-P.TRUSCIO/STRANGER.htm
* Honeybee information and activities: http://cals.arizona.edu/pubs/insects/ahb/lsn11.html
* Honeybee information: http://www.pbs.org/wgbh/nova/bees/hive.html

Lesson 12:
- Beetles Booklets: Answers found on pages 183 - 190
- Flies Booklet: Answers found on pages 190 - 192
- Mosquito Word Search Booklet: Find all of the words...they can go in any direction!
- True Bug Booklet: Answers found on pages 195 - 196

Additional Resources for Lesson 12:
* Information about mosquitoes: http://www.mosquitoes.org/educ_materials.htm
* Information about flies: http://www.nku.edu/~biosci/CoursesNDegree/ForensicFlyKey/flyanatomy.htm
* Really cute site about ladybugs: http://webtech.kennesaw.edu/jcheek3/ladybugs.htm
* When a bug is not an insect: http://www.sidney.ars.usda.gov/sidebar/justforkids2.html

Lesson 13:
- Praying Mantis Booklet: Answers found on pages 199 - 20
- Dragonflies & Damselflies Booklet: Answers found on pages 200 - 202
- Venn Diagram Booklet: Answers found on pages 203 - 207
- Aphids and Cicadas Booklet: 208 - 210

Additional Resources for Lesson 13:
* Information about Cicadas: http://saltthesandbox.org/cicada_hunt/
* Grasshopper Information: http://insected.arizona.edu/ghopperinfo.htm
* Cricket Information: http://insected.arizona.edu/cricketinfo.htm
* Praying Mantis Information: http://www.insecta-inspecta.com/mantids/praying/

Lesson 14:
- Life Cycle of a Butterfly Booklet: Answers found throughout the chapter
- Butterfly, Moth, Skipper Chart (Differences & Similarities) Booklet: Answers found throughout the chapter

Additional Resources for Lesson 14:
* Great Butterfly websites:
http://www.butterfly-guide.co.uk/help/parts.htm
http://www.shrewsbury-ma.gov/schools/beal/curriculum/butterfly/butterflies.html
http://www.primarygames.com/science/butterflies/facts.htm
* Butterfly wing patterns: http://www.bugbios.com/class/patterns/index.html

Additional Resources:

* "Bug Riddles" - http://www.uky.edu/Ag/Entomology/ythfacts/bugfun/riddles.htm
* Listen to some insect sounds! - http://www.naturesongs.com/insects.html
* Basic Insect Information: http://wings.avkids.com/Book/Animals/intermediate/insects-01.html
* Make paper-mache insects: http://www.uky.edu/Ag/Entomology/ythfacts/bugfun/papermch.htm
* Bug and Insect coloring pages: http://www.4kraftykidz.com/BugInsectcoloring.html
* Fun children's books about the topics of insects and bugs:

-Carle, Eric. The Very Quiet Cricket. This is a beautifully illustrated book with a wonderful surprise at the end (a chirping sound of a cricket) that children would enjoy reading over and over. It tells the story of a young male cricket that meets other insects but is unable to find its voice. Finally, upon meeting a female cricket, the young cricket is able to chirp the most beautiful chirp of all.

-Carle, Eric. The Very Hungry Caterpillar. This is another beautifully illustrated book by Eric Carle. It tells the story of a caterpillar that eats its way through the book until it turns into a beautiful butterfly. Children would love reading this story over and over.

- Carle, Eric. The Grouchy Ladybug. A wonderful tale about a ladybug who was so grouchy. The little bug always tries to fight with other animals but learns a valuable lesson in the end. It is full of beautiful colored illustrations and is a funny book to read aloud.

-Kent, Jack. The Caterpillar and the Polliwog. A humorous story about a caterpillar and her friend polliwog who turn into something different at the story's end. The caterpillar boasts about becoming a butterfly and becomes one, while the polliwog tries to become a butterfly too, but turns into a frog instead. This is a good story to tie into a science lesson about life cycles of insects or frogs.

-Maxner, Joyce. Nicholas Cricket. This is the story of a banjo-picking cricket named Nicholas. He plays in his "Bug-a-Wug" Cricket Band. It includes beautiful poetry and describes the grandness of the cricket's melodious tunes. This is a good story for children to read, though they need to know that Cricket Nick is no ordinary cricket.

* "Bug Games" online (interactive): http://www.scholastic.com/magicschoolbus/games/bugs/index.htm

**** Check our site for "Insect-Related" CopyWork!! www.knowledgeboxcentral.com

Flying Reptiles

Are they dinosaurs? Explain.

What does the Bible say about them?

```
P U P A S X N V D D M A J A F
M K L H Z I A V A U S S R V R
R T X H U H E P W G J N H O E
M S N I I T V S W I Q S P L S
E N P M A R F W E G G W A K T
L Y Q X J B I T E B P M U F I
V J E G I M B R A E E Z Z S E
K L A R V A C H P F U B X C F
O Y E B X D S T K V W T Q R L
Q X A P S Y W J N W Y Z K A Y
M T Z S P S E L W B Z D D T I
M O S Q U I T O A L P O T C N
S W A T Y F K D S O V Q P H G
I N S E C T T A D O P D J P H
I T C H H X M Z V D A D U L T
```

INSECT	FEMALE	PUPA	SCRATCH	FLYING
MOSQUITO	EGG	BITE	BLOOD	SWAT
ADULT	LARVA	ITCH		

Mosquito Word Search

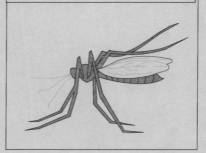

Insects

How to identify:

Why do we need them?

What does "cold-blooded" mean?

- Exoskeleton
- Molting
- Insect Heads
- Insect Eyes

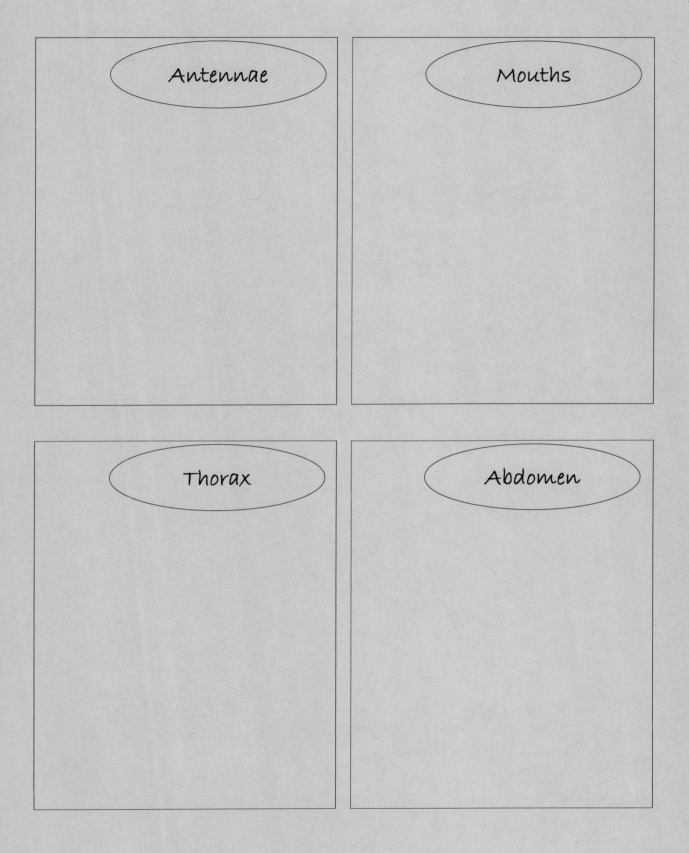

Lesson 8 Trivia

What makes a "bug" a TRUE BUG?

What is paleontology?

What part of a Pterosaurs' brain was very large?

What were a Pterosaurs' bones like?

Pterosaurs

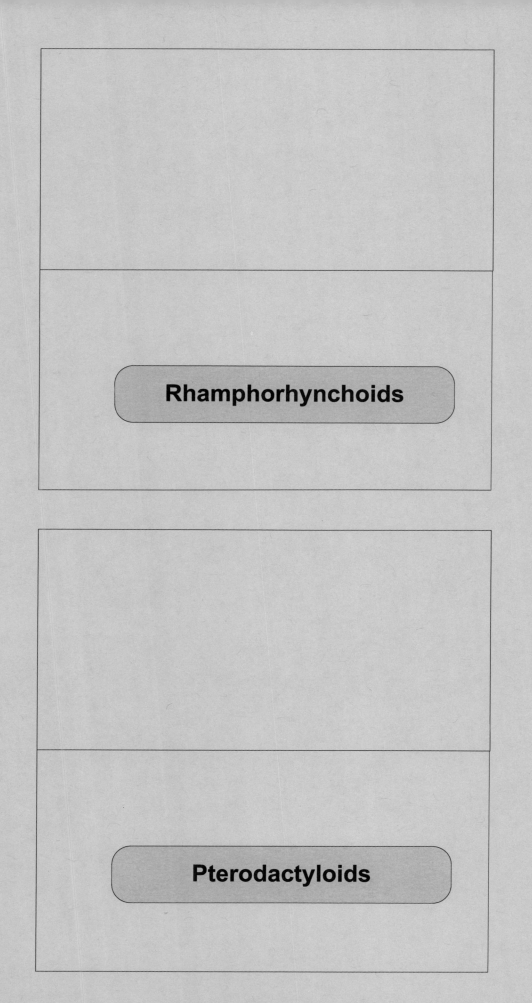

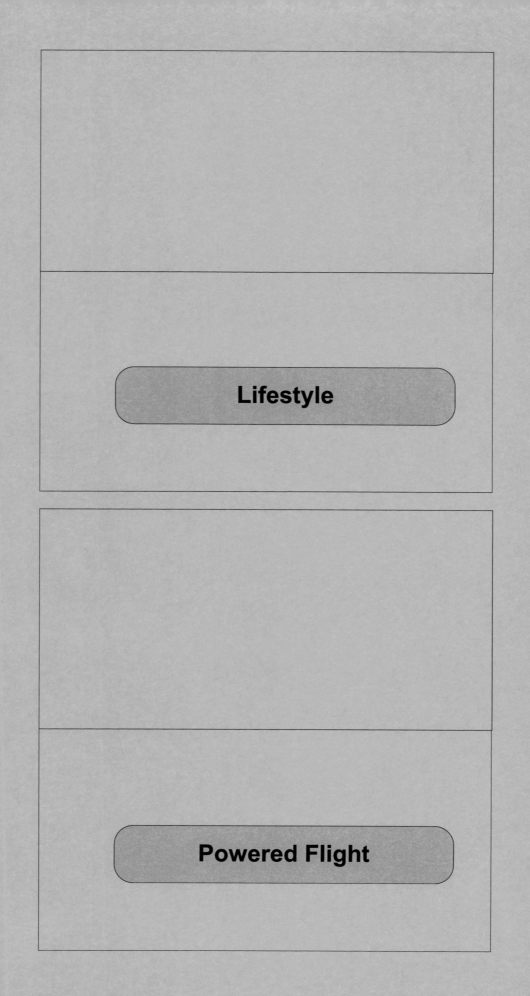

What is another name for the Praying Mantis?

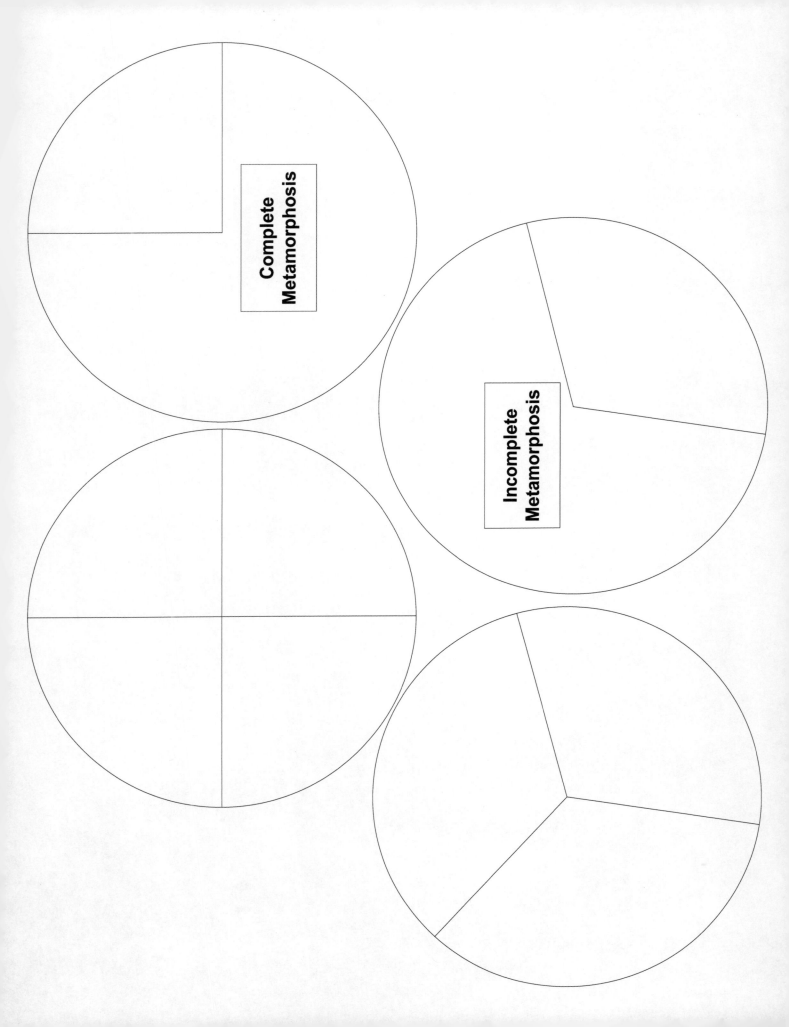

Megabats

Microbats

Lesson 9 Vocabulary

- Ovipositor
- Clasp
- Cerci
- Entomology

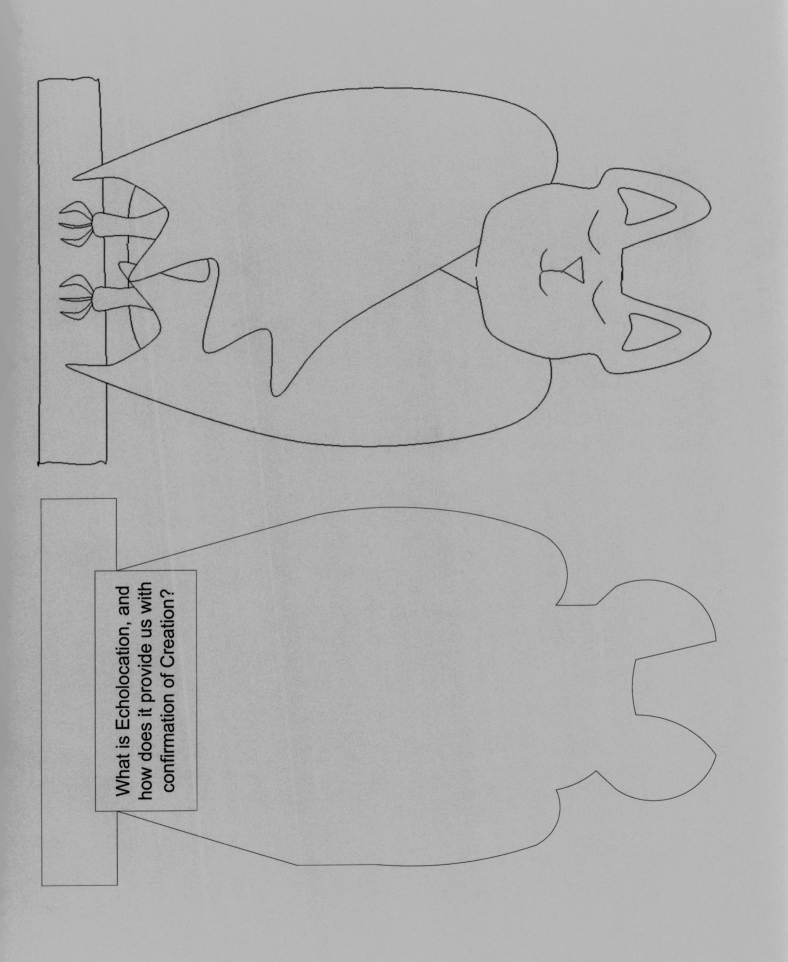

Name ways that an insect defends or protects itself.

Which Cicadas live for 2 years underground?

Which cicadas live for 17 years under the ground?

What is another name for Aphids?

What insect protects the Aphid?

Aphids & Cicadas

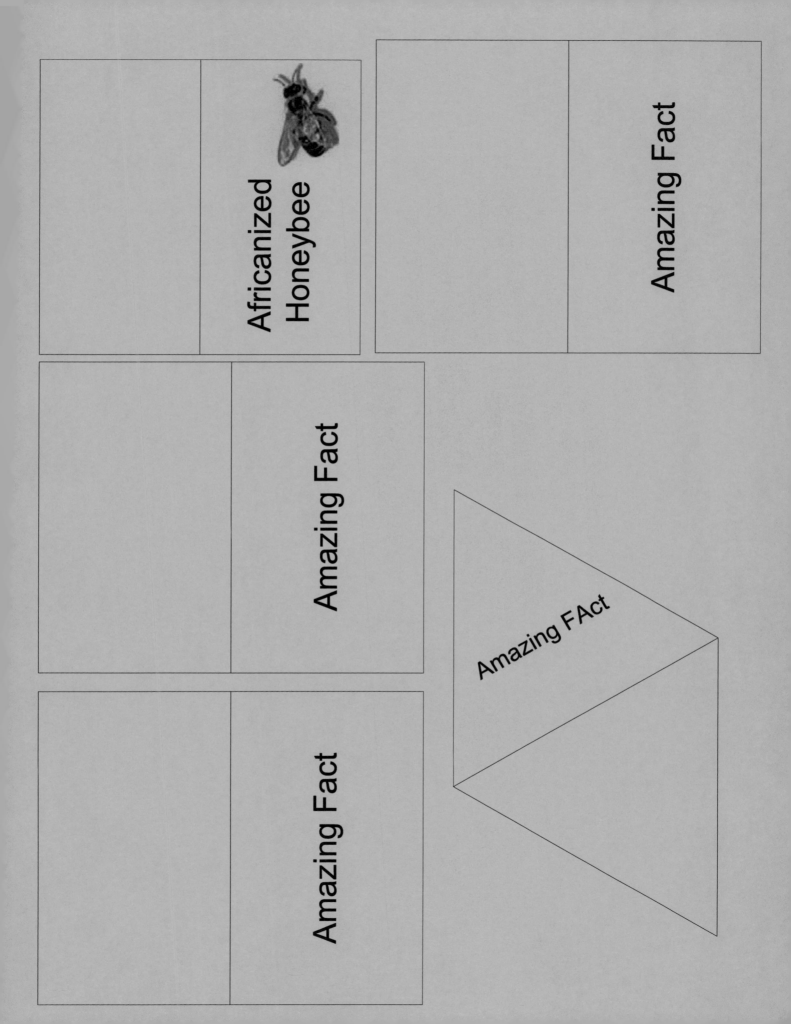

Flies

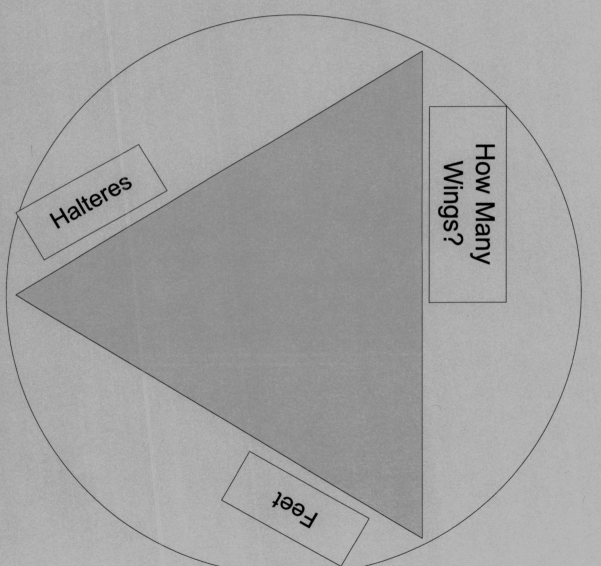

Halteres

How Many Wings?

Feet

Beneficial or Pesky?

Beetles

Ladybugs

Scarab Beetles

Beetle Behavior

Fireflies or Lightning Bugs

Bat Facts

What is interesting about bat hibernation & migration?

Name places where bats roost.

What beneficial tasks to bats perform?

How do mother bats care for their pups?

Social Insects Flashcard Game

How can you tell termites from ants?	What do social wasps make their nests out of?
How do termites give evidence of creation?	What is a solitary wasp?

Why is an ant bite so painful?	How are bumblebees different from honeybees?
Which type of ants have the hardest job in the colony?	What 3 things do gatherer bees collect from flowers?

Dragonflies and Damselflies

Wings	Eyes	Feeding	Describe their unique incomplete metamorphosis.

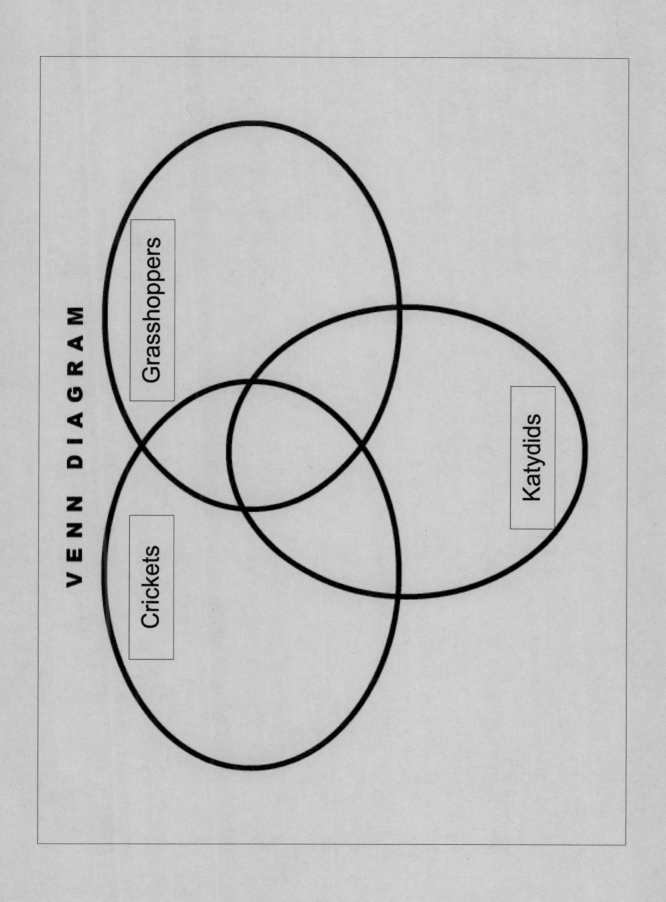

Lepidoptera	Antennae	Wings At Rest	Color
Butterflies			
Skippers			
Moths			

Do you know the differences and similarities?

Can you label the parts of the bat's anatomy?

The
Life Cycle
of a
Butterfly
(Can you place
them in order?)

Butterfly

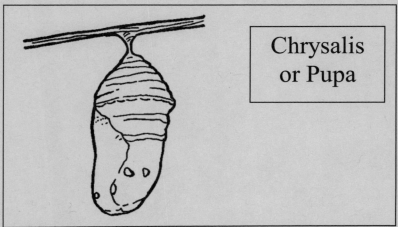

Chrysalis or Pupa

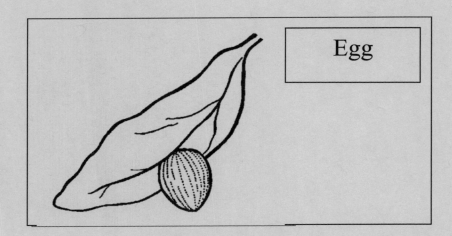

Egg

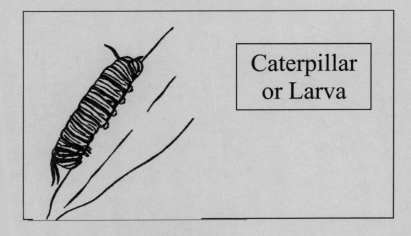

Caterpillar or Larva

Ants

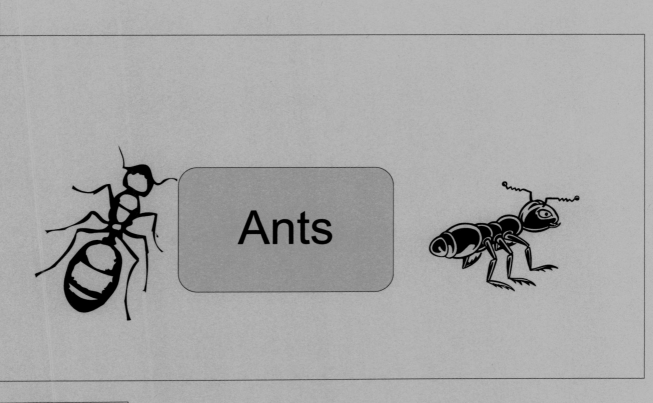

Queen, Drones, Alates

Worker Ants

Ant Talk

		Ant Food

		Shepherds & Farmers

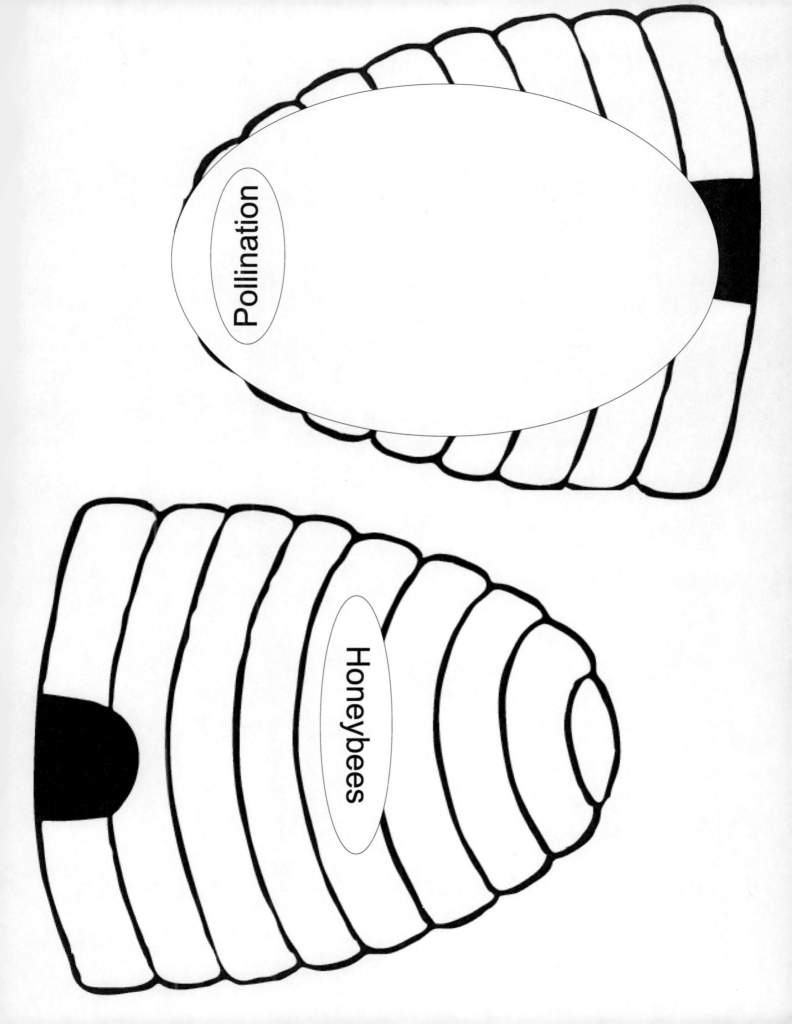

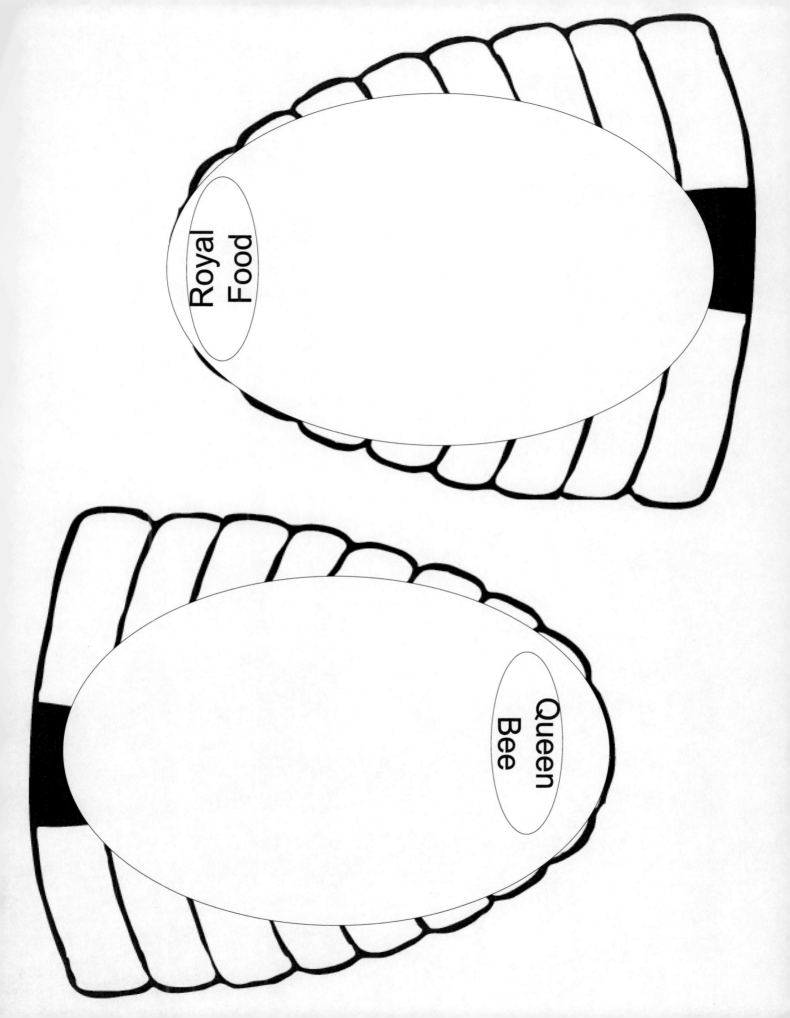

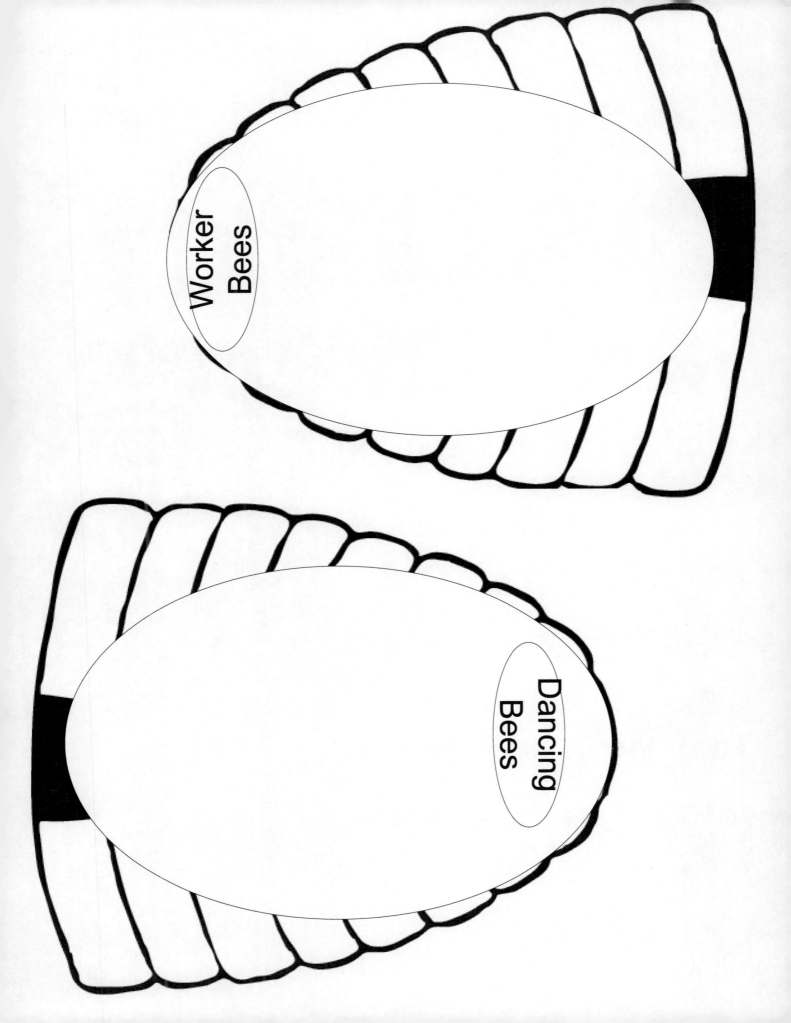